Onto the

Yellow School Bus

&

Through the Gates of Hell

Onto the

Yellow School Bus

&

Through the Gates of Hell

Mary Hood, Ph.D.

Cover Designed & Illustrated by

Art Gentry

Ambleside Educational Press

Onto the
Yellow School Bus &
Through the Gates of Hell

Published by Ambleside Educational Press
P. O. Box 2524
Cartersville, GA 30120

Cover art by Art Gentry

Printed in the U.S.A.
First printing

Printed on acid-free paper.

ISBN 0-9639740-3-3

"I am much afraid that the schools will prove the Gates of Hell unless they diligently labor in explaining the Holy Scriptures and engraving them in the hearts of youth. I advise no one to place his child where the Scriptures do not reign paramount. Every institution in which men are not unceasingly occupied with the Word of God must be corrupt."

- Martin Luther

Table of Contents

Preface

CHRISTIAN PARENTS: WAKE UP CALL!

A few years ago, I had a vivid dream. I was walking through a public elementary school with a group of building inspectors. Outside, ivy vines framed the entrance to the red brick structure. An American flag towered over the attractive landscape. School busses were beginning to arrive and several smiling teachers were lined up to escort the children to safety. A few parents were waiting to pick up their children after school, poking their heads out of their cars to wave and chat about the latest PTA fundraiser.

Inside, the inspectors were becoming increasingly agitated as they noted the condition of the interior of the building: sagging beams, ominous cracks in the ceiling, crumbling walls. I said to them, "We've got to warn the parents! The school is about to fall down. We have to get the children out!" "No! They shrieked. They mustn't know! We can't let them know!"

About that time, a few of the parents became concerned and wondered what was keeping their children. They started to approach the building, but it was too late. As we rushed out, it began to tumble down and the screams of the children could be heard above the roar and clatter of the falling timbers. Then there was silence. . .

The public school system of America is crumbling rapidly, because God's presence has been removed. It has been turned into a house built on sand, lacking His protection and blessing. Can it still be salvaged? Probably not. It certainly can't be fixed with a series of patching and repainting jobs. Only if the foundational problems themselves were cured would there be any hope at all. Due to the secular mind-set prevalent in America today, that's not very likely to happen.

Can you still save your own children? Of course you can. In fact, parents are probably the only people who really have the power to make the necessary changes. Nobody else can tell you what is right for your family, but this book will discuss several possible courses of action. You must take control of your children's education or face the consequences when the "experts" fail. Whatever you decide, you must do something soon if you don't want them to get caught by the falling timbers. It's not enough to read this book and nod your head in agreement. Do something, NOW. Tomorrow may be too late!

Part I:
First Things First

Chapter 1

Parents in Charge

This past weekend, our family joined thousands of others as we traveled over the river and through the woods to grandmother's house for Thanksgiving dinner. As usual, there wasn't much to do except catch up with relationships, eat too much food, and lay around on the sofa reading newspapers and old magazines. While playing couch potato, I came across an interesting article, written by a syndicated columnist. She had been forced to decline an assignment to write about the breakdown of the family unit, because she was too busy preparing Thanksgiving dinner for her relatives, caring for an aged parent, and taking her children to the dentist. She went on to discuss her belief that the American family has not declined at all. It has simply been redefined by newspaper editors and publishers. They have made us believe that the family is in trouble by constantly focusing on mothers that kill their children, fathers that hit their wives, and children that turn to drugs and alcohol because of dysfunctional relationships. She stated that such stories make the news precisely because they are sensational exceptions and create tantalizing headlines at the checkout line. They do not reflect what is going on in the majority of American families today.

I tend to agree with the author. The American family is not sinking beneath the waves. It may have changed character in some instances. There are certainly many more divorces today and more single-parent families than there were in days gone by. There are increasing problems with drugs, alcohol, and various forms of abusive behavior. Nevertheless, the family unit remains the cornerstone of American society. There has been one significant change over the years, however, even among the best of families. Most parents have given away their control and are no longer acting as captains of the ship. Rather, they have assumed roles as "ship's carpenters," trying to hold things together by patching and repairing rather than addressing the underlying problems and correcting their course. They have allowed their authority to be stolen and undermined by many thieves, including the television set and a sociological phenomenon called "peer pressure." The worst thief of all has been the public school system of America, which has robbed them of control over the best hours of their children's lives.

Our own family has been homeschooling for the past eleven years, but we considered entering the ranks of public school parents when our oldest son was due to enter the fourth grade. I spent an hour in the principal's office discussing Sam's proper academic placement, the teacher to whom he would be assigned, and the types of curriculum materials that would be used. At the end of the conversation, the principal smiled condescendingly and said to me, "Just remember Mrs. Hood, when your son begins school this fall, you won't be the one in charge anymore." I knew he was right. Like Peter Rabbit, I bolted for the door and didn't look back until I was safe in my cozy little home under the fir tree. There was no way I was prepared to give up that control to somebody else!

In my heart, I wish that all of you would get out of the public schools and become home schoolers, too. It's a wonderful life, and there's no better way to take back control of your children's lives than to educate them yourselves. I know that many of you don't want to do that right now. Maybe my story will encourage some of you to give it a try. I know that others will believe it is impossible for one reason or another. Just remember, the Bible states, *"The things which are impossible with men are possible with God"* (Luke 18:27). Most of the time our lifestyles are dictated by the decisions we make and the priorities we choose, either consciously or unconsciously. There are very few situations in which people truly have no choice at all.

Despite my love for homeschooling, however, I try hard not to be too judgmental. Maybe it isn't the life for you. You are the only ones who really know what will work best for your families. Whatever your own educational choices may be, they must reflect conscious decisions, made while on your knees asking God what is right for your individual family. It is time for you to stop allowing a bunch of educational "experts" to run your lives. *You* are the only experts that count when it comes to knowing your own children and what is best for them. It's not enough to raise funds for the PTA, bake cookies, reshelve books, help with bulletin boards or tutor children in the hallways. You have to get involved with the real educational process and insist on having a determining voice in decisions that matter. Only by realizing the power that you have as parents and using that power constructively can you can save your children from the destructive forces that are at work in the public schools today.

Chapter 2

Jesus at the Center

If Jesus is the Way, the Truth, and the Life, then we cannot be educating our children in truth if He is not at the center of their education. What a long way the public school system in America has come! Not only is Jesus not given His proper place at the center, but He has been banned from the periphery! If He were to come back tomorrow, and knock at the door, He wouldn't even be allowed in the classroom. Why? Because He wouldn't "sit on" His testimony. He wouldn't bow to an edict of the Supreme Court or listen to the latest dictates of the local school board. He wouldn't consider what was "politically correct," and He wouldn't give the other religions equal time. He would march right in and speak the truth boldly, the way He did at the temple in Jerusalem. He wouldn't come in at all, though, unless somebody opened the door first. He would wait until He was invited, because He respects the free will that has been given to His people. In this case, I'm afraid He'd have a long wait.

Contrary to popular belief, Jesus was not at the center of public education back in the "good old days," either. He was pushed off His throne at the conception of the public school system in the mid-1800s. It was set up as a secular institution from the start, meant to serve a pluralistic society. Of course, because control remained on a local level, there were many individual towns where Christian teachers, books, and ideas continued to dominate instruction. The top planners had something else in mind, however. These reformers were deliberately trying to eliminate the religious mentality of the citizens, and replace it with a secular mindset. In the beginning, many farsighted parents fought such an odd idea, but it gradually became an accepted fact of life. By the early 1900s, it was considered the normal course of action for children to leave their homes to become educated and socialized by so-called "experts" who could broaden their experiences and help them become more "enlightened" than their old-fashioned parents.

Like most transformations in society, this one occurred slowly, over the course of many years. In 1750, virtually all education in America was Christ-centered. By

1850, the secularists were hard at work trying to change that. In the 1950s, when I was a student in elementary school, Jesus was still allowed in the classroom, but he was "just one of the guys." Along with my classmates, I celebrated Christmas and Hanukkah with equal fervor. We played with spinning tops that the Jewish kids called "dreidels," and lighted a menorah together. Then we all turned around and sang Christmas carols. However, the Supreme Court decisions in the 1960s accelerated things drastically. Even multi-cultural religious experiences are usually denied to today's children. When I was a child, we had many different types of teachers. Some were Catholic, some Jewish, some Protestant. A few were probably atheist or agnostic, but they generally stayed quiet, because their ideas weren't popular back then. Those that were Christian weren't afraid to let their faith show in public. In the South, where my husband went to school, there were actually prayers over the intercom and Bible lessons every morning. We didn't have those things in Milwaukee, but they weren't absolutely forbidden, either.

As I write this, a debate is raging over whether or not to turn back the clock and legalize "school prayer." If the backers of the prayer amendment win, I will naturally applaud their efforts to restore a bit of religion to the public school classroom. However, a moment of prayer won't solve the underlying problem. William J. Murray, the former atheist whose mother filed the original suit banning school prayer, has been working hard to get it restored in the public schools. Even he concedes, however, that "putting one minute of prayer back in public schools will not, by itself, cure the ills of those schools or of our nation" (Wm. J. Murray Report, March 1995).

In the next section of this book, I'm going to be discussing spiritual warfare. The war that we are engaged in must be fought by many soldiers on a variety of fronts. Those Christians who are struggling to put prayer back into the public schools are fellow soldiers, and we share the same ultimate goals and purposes. However, I don't believe that their tactics are going to make a major impact. Unless this land is swept with revival, and the original intent of the nation's founders is completely restored, we are not going to be able to force the public school system to become a Christian system, with Jesus clearly at the center. We've gone too far toward an acceptance of plurality to do that. If we're not going to have a Christian school system, to whom will the children be praying? If the prayers are "dumbed down" as much as the textbooks, you can bet Jesus will never even be mentioned. I don't think that it is appropriate for Christian children to spend their time kneeling in front of a "politically correct" deity instead of the real thing.

Naturally, if the children want to pray silently over their school books, few teachers will try to stop them anyway. Some school districts are even experimenting with "moments of silence" expressly for this purpose. Since Christians are supposed to pray "in their closets," avoiding ostentatious piety, it might seem like the perfect solution. Unfortunately, these aren't mature Christians we're talking about. They are little children. When I was a child, a "moment of silence" would have served as a golden opportunity for the boy in the seat behind me to pull my braids through the inkwell. Without Christian adults around who are willing and able to guide these children toward the spiritual side of life, I doubt highly that many kids are going to have their minds on private worship sessions.

So it really all boils down to this. As long as Jesus is banished from His proper place at the center of your children's education, as long as the public schools remain secular institutions, committed to religious neutrality, Christian children don't belong there. It makes absolutely no sense for committed Christian parents to send their impressionable little sponges out, day after day, to spend their most productive hours in a place where Jesus isn't welcome. The "prayer issue" misses the whole point. Is Jesus in the center of your children's education or isn't He? If He isn't in His proper place, then you are not living up to your responsibility as parents. If your little children are sent off every day for the best part of their waking hours to a place where He isn't even allowed, then He can't be where He belongs. It just isn't enough to patch up and repair the problems when the kids come home at night. One Sunday morning a week, (or even three or four times a week) isn't nearly enough time to counteract the damage that is being done.

But where, you may ask, are the signs of damage? "My child is at a good school. The teachers are great! They are committed Christians, and the principal is a deacon at my church! We have test scores that are above the eightieth percentile in our state!   Our PTA is active, and we just finished the new wing to house the art and music departments! Besides, my children are acting as 'salt and light.' They are having a tremendous impact on their little classmates!"

Frankly, I doubt that last point, especially if the children are still in elementary or middle school. Most kids have a hard enough time maintaining their own standards in a tough situation. With a few possible exceptions, most children are not adequately prepared to serve as Christian soldiers in the middle of a battleground. They are out there trying to do the work of an adult with the mind and heart of a child. However, I can understand the source of your bewilderment. You may have a hard time agreeing with my assessment of the situation right now. I'm sure that some of you are justifiably proud of your local school districts. I have the highest respect for the many people who are out there trying to do the best job they possibly can under difficult circumstances. As long as there are any children remaining within the public system, they must never be abandoned. Mature Christians have the right and the responsibility to be out there fighting for the cause, but their own children just don't belong there anymore. You see, there's one major problem. Despite the efforts and good intentions of many committed men and women inside the system, the whole thing is being orchestrated by Satan himself!

When Jesus is moved out, there is never a void. There is no such thing as an education without values, without a center. There are two possible "centers" in this world, and without one, you have the other. The spiritual warfare in this world is reaching a climax, and Satan is clapping his hands with glee because the most fertile ground in America, the minds and souls of our children, has been handed to him on a platter.

The public schools of America have become "houses built on sand." The rains are coming and beating on those houses, and they are crumbling fast. Will you remove your children now and find another option? If you truly have no other option, will you cover them with your prayers and demand to be heard by the authorities on issues that matter? Or will you go off to work every day and leave them to enter those "Gates of Hell" unaided? You are their parents, and you are still the ones in charge, so make your choices wisely. It isn't my job to judge your decisions or your intentions, but there is Someone someday who will. Of course, He doesn't want you to turn to Him in fear, but to return to your children with love and joy and a renewed commitment to raise them under His authority, as He planned from the beginning.

Part II:

The Spiritual War Around Us

Chapter 3

Understanding Spiritual Warfare

The good guys versus the bad guys. White hats versus black hats. The force versus the dark side of the force. It's been the main theme of life and literature since the dawning of time. What exactly is spiritual warfare? Why does it appear to be escalating at this point in history, and what relevance does this topic have to the subject at hand?

When I was a child, my mother had a piece of advice that she repeated often. "Always stay in the middle of the road. Don't go to extremes." At the time, it sounded like a wise approach, but things have changed drastically in the intervening years. Evil has become much more blatant and accepted. "Frankly, Scarlett, I don't give a d---" has been replaced with things that used to make a sailor blush. Video stores feature posters dripping with blood and gore. Television shows, music albums, and fantasy games invite our children to participate in satanic rituals and solve their problems by committing suicide. If there ever was a middle road to travel, it no longer exists. The gap between good and evil is increasing every day, and it's necessary to choose paths deliberately or be swept along by forces outside our control.

I realize that some of you might not even believe in the reality of spiritual warfare, of angels and demons fighting each other for influence over your lives. At one point, I would have been skeptical myself. As is often the case, it took personal contact to open my eyes to this underlying reality.

When I was growing up, I witnessed my own father turn from a caring man with a wonderful sense of humor into someone who went for months at a time without speaking to his own family. Most people would have diagnosed him as mentally ill, but something more was going on. As an extremely intelligent person, he found it virtually impossible to set aside his "smarts" and accept a relationship with Jesus that was based on faith alone. He contemptuously referred to church people as "blind faith believers," and had me convinced at the age of ten that I could walk on water if I just "understood" as much as Jesus did.

His teachings would be called "new age" today. In his never-ending search for truth and peace, he gradually became more and more involved in his studies and started reading books on occultic subjects. In so doing, he opened the door to demonic attack.

When I was five, he was a wonderful daddy, bouncing me on his knee and carrying me around the room when I had too many pancakes to eat. When I was ten, he seemed very confused. Nothing was ever good enough to please him and he was constantly arguing and complaining. By the time I was twenty, he looked gray and ashen, and walked around shaking his head like he didn't know what to do anymore. Weeks of silence were punctuated by bouts of irrational behavior. Finally he died, in his early sixties, leaving behind a daughter who had to spend years trying to forgive him for the man he had become.

As a young adult, I had two influences in my life. On the one hand, my mother had never stopped believing in Jesus through the bad years, and had often left literature around on the table that helped point me in the right direction. I certainly considered myself a Christian in those days, although I couldn't figure out why I was supposed to be a "sinner." I thought I was doing pretty well on my own.

On the other hand, I inherited my father's intelligence and quest for knowledge, and began searching in some of the same places he did. I read books on reincarnation, and experimented with having "out-of-body" experiences. One time I was lying in bed, purposefully opening my mind to spiritual influences, and wound up wrestling with an unseen force until it threw me onto the floor. That was my first experience with a demonic attack. Although I didn't recognize it at the time, it scared the heck out of me, and I stopped consciously experimenting with such forces.

As the years passed, I continued to walk in two worlds. With one ear, I listened to the "700 Club," and went to church with my Christian husband, considering myself a bastion of spirituality. With the other ear, I kept on listening to the other side, constantly searching for other possible answers. Despite developing a true yearning for Christ's presence in my life, I kept a large crack in the door open for the devil's influence.

That was the situation when I was a young mother. Most of the time, I appeared to be a staunch Christian, who seemed to have everything together. Once in awhile, though, my temper would flare or I would get extremely moody. The world might have attributed this to PMS, or diagnosed me as "manic-depressive," but I knew the problem went deeper than that. When I would get in one of my moods, I would sometimes come close to abusing those close to me. A force much stronger than I seemed to temporarily take control. I wanted to change, to be different, to be a better mother, but I couldn't seem to make any permanent changes on my own.

In the early 1980s, I finally took the step that I'd been avoiding so long. I had a vision in which I saw myself standing in a doorway. On one side, there was a bright light. The other side was pitch dark. I had one foot firmly planted in each side, and recognized that it was time to make a choice. Very deliberately, I pulled my other foot into the bright room.

Almost immediately, I began to meet people who wanted to discuss spiritual warfare. One of my friends loaned me a book on the subject and I began to study it intensely. I learned that spiritual warfare is just what it sounds like. Satan and his demons are fighting God and His angels for control of the universe. Luckily, we already know Who will win. Satan knows, too, and it just makes him want to fight harder. He realizes he is already defeated, and he wants to bring down as many people as possible while there's still time.

Many Christians with a sincere faith in Jesus don't seem to recognize the reality of Satan. Just as it takes a personal relationship with Jesus to really know Him and recognize His voice, it takes personal contact with Satan to become aware of him as a living being and to recognize the suggestions that emanate from his side. Those of you who know Jesus, but haven't "met" Satan can be grateful for the shield that has protected you. I didn't always have that shield. I know through personal experience that Satan is just as real as Jesus, and that he is infinitely more powerful than human beings. We aren't strong enough to fight his influence by ourselves, but when we call on Jesus and repudiate any occultic influences we have allowed into our lives, Satan is obligated to flee. Powerful though he may seem by human standards, he cowers in the presence of the Lord.

When I first began to understand the source of the problems I had been experiencing as a young mother, I had a lot of "repudiating" to do. I had to get rid of all my books on reincarnation and my posters on astrology. I had to stop thinking of myself as a "typical Leo," and stop reading the daily horoscope in the paper. I had a lot of sins to confess, grudges to release, and hurts to forgive. Gradually, as I stood up to Satan in the name of Jesus, I developed the ability to discern the source of the evil suggestions that had been dragging me down and to be victorious over them.

In order to achieve victory, it is necessary that you also recognize the reality of this source of evil. If there are any occultic materials in your house, get rid of them immediately. Many items that you might not even notice have satanic overtones. Most of you are already aware of the devilish content of some rock lyrics or videos, but they aren't the only offenders. "Innocuous" children's games, like "Dungeons and Dragons," can be the worst. Even seemingly innocent cartoon characters can have occultic origins. Above all, any books or materials on the occult, witchcraft, astrology, and reincarnation must be eliminated from your bookshelf, and kept out of your children's hands. Practices such as "automatic writing," "out-of-body experiences," "tarot card reading," and playing with a "ouija board" must be stopped and the sins connected with them must be confessed. As long as the door is kept open a crack, Satan has a way to enter and has your implied permission to influence the thoughts and actions of your household.

Once he has gained entrance, Satan loves to stir up your worst emotions. One of the most effective tools he has used against me has been my own overactive imagination. Once I was driving down the road, and a car swerved toward our van. Instead of saying, "Thank God we're safe," my mind immediately brought up a vivid image of what could have happened, complete with blood and gore and dismembered bodies. One simple suggestion and my mind used to go off on a tangent. Since I have turned to Jesus for help, such attacks come less often. Once in awhile, though, Satan still tries to hassle me and take away my joy and peace. When that happens, it takes a deliberate effort to recognize where such suggestions originate and repudiate them before they can take over my emotions and ruin my day completely.

Demons can also use our weaknesses, tempers, and vanities as starting points to wreak their foul-minded havoc. One of my own biggest stumbling blocks on the road to spiritual maturity was a continuing hatred for my father and the feeling of unworthiness that resulted from his apparent disdain for me. As I learned more about spiritual warfare, it gradually dawned on me that it was really his actions and the demons that were controlling them that I hated. I began to be able to separate my feelings for them from the emotions I felt for the man inside, and was finally able to understand and forgive him. As I did so, the vise that had held me in its grip for so many years loosened and was no longer able to hurt me. At this point, I can honestly say that I love my father and pray for his well-being. There was a time I wouldn't have believed it was possible.

Although I've come a long way over the years, I am still not immune from demonic attack. None of us are. Even now, when I'm about to do something special for God, like teach a workshop at a secular university, or write a book or an article, I can sense that Satan is trying once again to trip me and render me ineffective. He doesn't give up easily. Satan can't control me anymore, though, because I recognize him for what he is now and just say "No." I suppose it makes him pretty mad.

****

So what does all this personal rambling have to do with the state of the public school system? Just this: It's absolutely critical that you open your eyes to the spiritual warfare going on around you if you want to really understand the underlying problems in today's world, especially in the area of public education. With God removed from the picture, Satan has been having an absolute field day.

In this book, I'm not going to present a litany of problems that affect today's school children, because you can read about them in any magazine or newspaper you pick up. Violence is increasing. Drug problems are proliferating. Teenagers are committing suicide, performing unspeakable acts of sexual perversion, and participating in crimes that were unheard of a few decades ago. These problems are complex, and the surface causes are many:

- Parents who don't care or aren't at home enough...
- A curriculum that undermines traditional morality...
- Television producers who care more about money than they do about their influence on the young people of today...

The list goes on and on. But the underlying cause is generally the same. Satan is on the prowl, especially in the public school system. He is doing everything he can to destroy our young people and drag them down into the dirt where he wants them to live and die and ultimately join him in Hell.

At this point, I can hear parents all over America saying, "She's right. This is awful. Something needs to be done... Thank God she isn't talking about *my* child's school!" ... But I *am* talking about your child's school! This book is addressed to all of you, not just to parents in the big city ghettos.

Okay, maybe you don't see guns or knives in your child's school yet. Maybe the drugs do appear to be limited to a few troublemakers. Maybe your child's teacher this year is a committed Christian and your principal is a wonderful man. It doesn't change a thing. It's *your* school I'm talking about. If it is built on sand, it has no foundation and cannot continue standing indefinitely. With Jesus banished and Satan free to roam, your teachers and principals are fighting a losing battle. Most of them know it in their hearts, even if some of them don't realize what the underlying problem is. Did you know that a very large percentage of home-schooling parents are either former or current teachers in the public school system? Many of them recognize that all the educational reforms and parent involvement programs and student awareness retreats in the world aren't going to do anything but patch things temporarily and put on a new coat of paint. The real changes that need to be made are not likely to be forthcoming. That's the reason that so many of these teachers leave the system when their own children reach school age so they can work with them one to one at home.

For those of you who aren't currently in the public school arena, it's important to realize that Satan can come around and hassle you and your children, too. As a matter of fact, I think that he is very upset with the booming home-schooling movement, because he doesn't like having all those potential souls removed from "his" school system. Home-schooling parents and children certainly aren't immune from his attacks, and neither are private school students. Unless people recognize his activities and repudiate them in the name of Jesus, anyone can succumb anywhere, at any time.

As a home-schooling consultant, I've had an increasing number of letters from mothers who are ready to throw in the towel, citing PMS, stress, money problems, and everything else under the sun. A number of committed Christian friends have recently toyed with the idea of divorce. Where do you suppose these ideas are coming from? Who do you think is responsible for the sudden increase in "problems" that are interfering with the ability of these parents to maintain a stable home life?

If any of you fear that satanic influences are at work in your own lives or are trying to grab your children's allegiance, the first thing to do is to begin praying for yourselves and your children in earnest. If possible, gather a group of concerned Christians and do it together. Surround the people you love with an armor of your faith, and ask the angels to come help your children when you aren't around. My mother might not have understood about spiritual warfare when I was growing up, but I'm convinced that her prayers kept me safe during the years when I was dabbling in the occult, doing drugs, and running around with a dangerous crowd.

The second thing to do, of course, is to discover the source of any "crack" in your family's armor, to eliminate any occultic materials or practices, and to ask forgiveness for your sins. If you or any members of your family were abused as children, and those abusers were involved in the occult themselves, you may also have "inherited" negative spiritual influences. Repudiate them in Jesus' name, and ask the Lord to help you forgive those who have sinned against you in the past.

You can't be successful in battle until you understand the nature and strength of the enemy forces. You can't win unless you are adequately prepared, and have the Lord squarely on your side. Ephesians 6:1-18 tells what you must do if you want to win the war for your children:

> *Put on the whole armour of God, that ye may be able to stand against the wiles of the devil. For we wrestle not against flesh and blood, but against principalities, against powers, against the rulers of the darkness of this world, against spiritual wickedness in high places. Wherefore take unto you the whole armour of God, that ye may be able to withstand in the evil day, and having done all, to stand. Stand, therefore, having your loins girt about with truth, and having on the breastplate of righteousness; and your feet shod with the preparation of the gospel of peace. Above all, taking the shield of faith, wherewith ye shall be able to quench all the fiery darts of the wicked. And take the helmet of salvation, the sword of the Spirit, which is the word of God, praying always with all prayer and supplication in the Spirit..."*

So stand fast, clad in the appropriate armor, and begin praying for your children. They are little lambs whose Shepherd has been driven away. Ask the Lord what He wants you to do, and then act on His answer. If, for some reason, you can't bring them away from the front lines immediately, at least join them there and cover them with your shield. Don't leave them to face the "angry wolf" all alone!

Chapter 4

Recognizing Spiritual Influences

There are several important things to understand before you start trying to identify demonic influences or point fingers at individual people or trends. There are at least three levels of demonic activity. There is true demonic possession, where a person has experimented with the occult so much that he has allowed himself to be completely taken over by outside forces. Once such possession has occurred, the person totally loses control, and can't help himself without outside intervention. The best example of this in the Bible is the wild man in the graveyard, who had to be chained in order to protect other people. He is the one whose demons were eventually driven out into a herd of pigs.

In recent times, I am convinced that Adolf Hitler was possessed. Did you ever hear him speak? His voice sounded like shrieking. He was responsible for hideous experimentation on human beings, as well as the torture, deprivation, and execution of thousands of innocent women, children, and babies. I'm sure that was a case of demonic possession. It makes me wonder what would have happened if Jesus had been around to tell his demons where to go. It probably would have taken fifty herds of pigs to get rid of all those evil spirits!

The second level of demonic influence is "oppression," where a person maintains his or her own identity, but is oppressed or "hassled" by demonic forces. Such oppression can vary in degrees of severity. My own situation was a mild form of oppression, while some people have it much worse.

The third level of demonic influence is probably the most prevalent. This is where good-hearted, decent people are unwittingly used by Satan to further his plans and goals. Many of the satanic influences in the public schools are the result of this type of "innocent" cooperation with Satan's agenda. Any teachers, parents, school board members, principals, or students who do not recognize and reject the negative spiritual forces present in today's world can be used in this manner, whether they call themselves Christians or not.

In all of these cases, it is important to make a distinction between demonic influences and the people who are being influenced or used for evil purposes. Remember, this is a spiritual war that is raging. We are supposed to be fighting the underlying spiritual influences through a combination of work and prayer. The human players are our brothers and sisters, the children of God. Regardless of their current lifestyles, God has told us to love them and accept them exactly as they are right now, just like He does. (That doesn't mean we should accept their actions or beliefs, though!) Only through love and prayer can the demonic influences be beaten and the people won over. It doesn't help at all to call them names and point our fingers at them.

Also keep in mind that, in addition to the negative spiritual influences at work, there are an equal or greater number of positive spiritual influences active in the world today. For every demon that is hanging around to bother you and give you foul-minded suggestions, there is an angel waiting to protect you and help you fight your battles. However, these angelic beings don't come in automatically to help. Just like Jesus, they respect human free will, and don't usually make a move unless they have been clearly invited to participate in a person's life. That's one of the biggest reasons that it's so important for parents to cover their young children with constant prayer. This is particularly true when those children are out in a secular environment all day where they are susceptible to negative influences.

For those of you who want to develop the ability to discern spirits and recognize their presence, it is possible to do so. The first prerequisite, though, is to be a "Spirit-filled Christian." It is not enough to believe in Jesus in order to be able to understand this spiritual war. You must also ask to be filled with the Holy Spirit, in order to tap into His power source and have your eyes opened to the realities of this unseen world. Even Jesus' own disciples were instructed not to go out to share his message until they had received the Holy Spirit. Without that power, it is impossible to teach or preach effectively, or to receive "supernatural" knowledge or insight.

Some people have a major spiritual experience when they receive the Holy Spirit, seeing bright lights or speaking in tongues. Others receive Him more quietly. My own conversion and filling with the Spirit was one of the most gradual in history. I never did have a "Damascus road experience." I simply grew in joy and understanding until it became obvious that certain gifts were mine. Since that time, I have often experienced the power inside. Writing this book is a classic example. Every morning I sit down at the computer, and the words simply flow onto the paper. I may be a pretty good writer, but this is the first book I haven't had to research, outline, and plan in advance! Before I received the Holy Spirit, I wasn't even able to share my faith with my own family. I felt like I was walking around with a clamp on my tongue. The fact that I can now write for a national audience is proof enough for me that the power is coming from the Holy Spirit, rather than from my own abilities and talents.

Chapter 5

Fighting Back

There's an old hymn that begins, "Onward Christian Soldiers, marching as to war, with the cross of Jesus going on before."

If we are going to win this spiritual war, we have to start acting like a group of disciplined soldiers for Christ. The words of the song show us where to begin: "We are not divided, all one body we, one in hope and doctrine, one in charity."

There has been far too much in-fighting among Christians. The Catholics fight the Protestants. Traditional believers don't want to hang around with charismatics. Folks at the Baptist convention thrive on arguing with each other, breaking up into factions and splitting hairs. It's amazing anybody gets anything accomplished at all for the kingdom.

Even within the Christian segment of the home-schooling movement, people with similar religious views quarrel with each other over questions of curricula and methodology. Satan must be extremely delighted when he sees all these Christians spending their energies on attacking each other rather than fighting the real enemies of the faith.

While there are valid doctrinal differences among the various Christian sects, it seems awfully judgmental when one group refers to others as if they aren't even Christians. As someone who grew up in a cosmopolitan community, and had a lot of Catholic friends, it particularly bothers me when I see people putting Catholics on the same level as "New Agers" or "Satanists." Being a Christian is not a question of being a Lutheran or a Catholic or an Episcopalian. No single denomination has a monopoly on being saved. The only question that really counts is whether or not a specific person has genuinely given his or her heart to Jesus. There are many people who go to church every Sunday who aren't really part of Jesus' flock. On the other hand, there are many people who remain outside the church that have truly turned their lives over to Christ. That's an individual question, and one that is past our finite ability to judge. If someone tells me that he or she is a Christian, that's all that matters to me. As far as I'm concerned that person is on my side. I know that I can trust the Holy Spirit to reveal the truth to me if I need to be shown otherwise.

When Corrie Ten Boom first started her underground work in Holland during World War II, she was concerned that she didn't know the political or spiritual beliefs of the people she needed to contact for help. Then it dawned on her that, while she didn't know their leanings, God did! It was enough to ask for His guidance in pointing out the people who would be willing to help. If we sincerely ask for His assistance in determining who should be trusted in this spiritual war, He will let us know. We don't have to attempt to do the judging for Him. That's not our business.

Back in Maryland, where I used to live, there was a church that was too dogmatic for my personal tastes. Some of the leaders also tended to deny the gifts of the Holy Spirit that I personally believed in. When it came to something important, however, we were able to set aside our doctrinal differences and work together for the cause.

One of the members, who was a personal friend of mine, called to warn me of a book in the library that she found offensive. At first, I didn't really warm up to the idea of fighting the librarians. My own kids were volunteers there. We spent a lot of time in the library and relied on many of their materials for our home-schooling work. Besides, I've never considered myself a "book censor." Naturally, I insist on certain standards, and won't allow occultic materials to be brought into the house. However, I've always allowed my children to read a wide variety of materials, especially works that are considered "classics." I always make sure that I know the content of the books they are reading. If there are any objectionable sections, we discuss them together. I also realize that the public library, like the public school, is set up to serve a pluralistic society. If we want our Christian books to remain on the shelves, we have to understand that certain other books which offend our tastes will also be allowed in. Once in awhile, I've taken a book on witches or reincarnation from a prominent display and reshelved it to get it out of the public eye, but that was as radical as I'd been up to that point.

The next time I went to the library, however, I decided to check out the book for myself. What I found was appalling. The book looked like a "baby-sitter's club" book, designed to attract a middle-school audience. The front cover featured a picture of a young child swinging, and it was located on the "new book" counter, directly across from the check-out aisle, where any child might be tempted to pick it up. The name of the book was, *Getting Jesus in the Mood*. To be fair to the author, whose intentions I do not aim to judge, it was not supposedly meant to be a children's book. It was designed for adult audiences, and dealt with a woman's attempts to put a lifetime of abuse behind her. However, as I started to read the book, I felt the Holy Spirit rise up and become outraged. The author discussed such topics as a young girl having sexual fantasies with the devil and with Jesus Christ, and also contained a story of a baby-sitter having sexual experiences with a small child. It was obviously not something you would want your middle-school-aged daughter to pick up and take home. As I sat there in the library, reading certain sections, I felt the Holy Spirit's wrath in a way I had never felt it before. Frankly, it scared me. I was a little afraid the entire library was about to blow up, and reminded God that my daughter and I were inside. After I went home, He guided me to a passage of the Bible that discussed how God's wrath is reserved for people who ignore His teachings, and was not directed at us.

I decided to join forces with my friends from the other church and try to have the book removed from the library (or at least placed in a less obvious area). We got together a coalition of Christians from a variety of different churches and began a petition and letter-writing campaign. We also approached our legislators to express our concern about tax monies being used for such materials. When we asked the library board members to consider removing the book from the library, we learned something rather distressing. Their policy was to choose books solely on their literary merit. There was absolutely no provision for removing books because the content offended the standards of the community. In fact, their policy clearly indicated that if a segment of the population was disturbed by the values orientation of a book, that book was obviously "controversial," which they equated with "popular and needed." Consequently, the end result of such a campaign would probably be a decision to buy more copies for their branches!

Nevertheless, our battle was not a complete loss. The book was taken off the "new book" shelf, and retired to a less conspicuous place in the adult section. For several weeks, the local newspaper was full of letters concerning the issue. If a few of the Christians in the area had their eyes opened to the problem, at least something important was gained. Even the librarians told us that they were "happy for the dialogue." It probably was the most publicity their library had enjoyed in a long time.

The experience taught me a valuable lesson. With the public schools on the decline, part of our effort as Christians should be devoted to trying to keep the public libraries from going the same direction. Most libraries are not as far down the road toward demonic influence as their corresponding school systems. Although there are certainly many occultic books on the shelves, there are also still a great many Christian books to balance them. God may not be in charge in the public library, but at least He has not yet been banned. Christian librarians are still able to exert influence through their jobs and Christian parents are still allowed to request books that fit their own value systems. It's our job to continue monitoring the situation, to make sure our presence and opinions count. If we give up and throw in the towel, we may wind up having to form a new system of Christian libraries in a few years. I'd rather try to save the libraries and devote our attentions to creating a new system of Christian education!

As end times approach, the chasm between good and evil will become larger and larger. Both sides will grow in power. The evil will intensify beyond anything we are seeing today. The good will also shine through, as revival begins to sweep the world in preparation for Jesus' Second Coming. Although it is necessary to recognize and repudiate the evil forces around us, there's no need for us to be afraid. God is infinitely more powerful than Satan, and His power is there for us to tap into anytime we ask.

"For God has not given us the spirit of fear, but of power, and of love, and of a sound mind" (2 Timothy 1:7).

With Jesus on your side, nothing is impossible. Nothing Satan throws at you or your children will ever be able to conquer you! There is literally nothing left to be afraid of! Stand up and fight! Your children need your help NOW!

Part III
A Strategy for Change

Chapter 6

The Battle for Our Children

Before the public school system was created in America, most American education was church-related. Beginning with the Puritans, who set up schools as soon as they arrived in order to teach their children to read the Bible, virtually all education was religious in nature. Young children either went to small church schools or were taught or tutored at home. Older children either served apprenticeships or went to universities like Harvard, which were, at the time, run by the church.

From the very start, the creators of the public school system had a distinctly different agenda. The public school was set up as a secular institution which would gradually remove the presence of God and replace Him with a new "enlightened" view of mankind. Early "visionaries," like Horace Mann, saw the schools as a way to "broaden" the scope of education, and create a new group of citizens who were more open-minded and less dogmatic than their forefathers.

At the beginning, most public schools on the frontier still seemed a lot like Christian schools because they were kept under local control. Since the majority of the residents were often Christians, they selected Christian teachers and used materials that taught reading by starting, "A.. In Adam's fall, we sinned all."

The slide into decay took place subtly and gradually, over a hundred and fifty years. Parents began to fall for the idea that their children were best educated by "experts." Small local schools were replaced by large consolidated schools and children were bussed away from their residential neighborhoods. The federal government began to step in and interfere with decision-making on the local level. During this time, a small group of influential educators had an agenda that was definitely satanic in origin, whether they realized it or not. In *The Humanist Manifesto,* some of these leaders clearly spelled out their desire to replace God with a "humanist philosophy" that placed man at the center, rather than Jesus. The individual teachers and principals were not the ones responsible for the underlying decisions that gradually moved the public school further and further toward the edge. However, they may at times have allowed themselves to be used as unwilling or unknowing "pawns" in the war.

The Supreme Court ruling that removed God and school prayer from the public schools was the end result of many years of movement in that direction. That trend was not created overnight by a few judges in a back room. However, once the decision was handed down, Satan's forces were enabled to move into the forefront, since their main adversary had been plainly told He was no longer welcome. It is no coincidence that violence has increased, drug use has escalated, discipline has collapsed, and test scores have declined in the years since God has been banned from the classroom.

Someone once said that if you become too open-minded, your brains may fall out. That is a good description of what has been happening in the public educational sphere over the years. It has gradually become an accepted "fact" that the more educated a person is, the less his faith is supposed to matter. Many people have expressed astonishment that I was able to maintain my Christian beliefs during my long career as a student. They expected me to follow the lead of the other students and teachers, who took a different road. As the Bible says, *"Professing themselves to be wise, they became fools"* (Romans 1:22).

In an effort to turn out students who are "broad-minded," the public schools have emphasized the teaching of "relative morality" instead of traditional morality. There are no more absolutes, according to the authorities in question. Instead, what is right depends on the specific situation. Young children are given lessons in "values clarification," where they are systematically taught to ignore the teachings of their parents and make their own decisions. Yet they are not really encouraged to make their own individual choices, but to form a "consensus," by discussing the issues with their peers. Thus, seven year olds are being taught by other seven year olds, who are all fashioning a "new" ideal of right versus wrong that does not mesh with the belief systems of their parents.

There are many ways in which satanic influences are coming into the schools. Students are allowed, or even encouraged, to play fantasy games like "Dungeons and Dragons," which lead them directly into contact with demonic influences. Books can be found in the library on subjects which are clearly demonic in nature, and would never have been allowed twenty years ago. Teachers lead the children in meditation under the pretense of "stress reduction."

In a college course where I was being trained to be a teacher of small children, we were asked to participate in such an experience. We were told to put our heads on our desks, visualize a green meadow with a stream running through it, relax completely, and then have a conversation with a "friend" who came to see us in the meadow. This type of experience is about as "New Age" as you can get. I told the teacher that I was not going to participate because I didn't think it was an appropriate exercise for a Christian. To his credit, he allowed me to abstain. However, every other person there did participate and was trained to initiate similar stunts with their primary-aged students later on.

Four years ago, my husband and I spent three months in close association with a public middle school. Our oldest son was then in the seventh grade, and he had convinced us to let him give public school a try. (That was before we became convicted about the subject, obviously). By Christmas break, Sam decided he wanted to come back home. If he had wanted to remain, we would have probably required that he return home, anyway. Three months as public school parents were all that we could stand!

At one point during his stint in public school, Sam's class was doing book reports. Because the teacher knew I was an educator, she proudly told me that the class was using a "hands-on approach." That sounded great until I found out that one of the books they were reading was *The Seance,* and the students had actually gone through the motions of having a seance during the book report in question!

Another time I was invited to come to the school to "preview night," where the parents were given the opportunity of seeing the audiovisual materials selected for the sex education class. When I got there, I couldn't help but notice that only twelve parents had cared enough to come. We were shown a film strip that explained human reproduction. It kept going back and forth between diagrams of sexual organs and pictures of a boy and girl necking in a car. Apparently they were going to teach the middle schoolers using a "This is what it is and this is what you do with it" approach!

Next, we watched a video about sexually transmitted diseases. A young girl was told she had a serious disorder that could eventually render her sterile and possibly cause death. She had gone to a school clinic and was speaking to a nurse about the problem. At the end, the nurse asked the girl if she had any other concerns. "I'm just afraid of what my parents will say when they find out!," the girl sobbed. "Oh, we don't have to tell them," was the nurse's response.

At the conclusion of the video, the person in charge asked if anyone had any concerns about the materials. A few parents looked a little dazed, but they all said things like, "Well, we're not really experts on this. If you think it's okay, it probably is." Not one parent complained about the obvious anti-family values expressed in the video. Not one parent publicly asked to have their child excused from the sex class. Of course, neither did I! I wasn't always this bold, you see!

Afterwards, I did go to the nurse in private and told her my son would not be participating. I said, "By the way, I realize that you think you can't actually teach Judeo-Christian morality because of the Supreme Court decisions, but do you ever tell the children they shouldn't "make babies" before marriage because it is <u>wrong</u>, or just because it is "inconvenient?" Her response was, "Oh, we can't get into the area of values."

Anyone that thinks you can teach things like sex education and drug education while staying completely away from the area of values has been deluded and is being "used" by Satan. There is no such thing as education without values. If you aren't teaching one set then you are teaching the other.

If, after reading this book, you still feel that your children must stay in the public school arena, you must realize that you are allowing them to stand on the front lines of a spiritual war. The war itself may already be won, but the individual battles are still up for grabs. In order to be the victor, you've got to be willing to fight on their behalf. You've got to attend meetings, speak your mind, and exercise your right to have your children excused from such programs. The fact that only twelve parents attended that meeting out of several hundred says a lot about the real reason for the deterioration of the public school system. Local control of the schools has slipped away precisely because concerned parents have bowed out of the picture.

The main thrust of this book, however, is not "what to do if your children stay in the public schools." I believe that God wants us all to take our children out <u>now</u>. There's more than one way to win a war. Sometimes a planned retreat can be more effective than a frontal assault. It's high time that we develop other alternatives and establish a whole new system of education that has Him at the center. We need to start with fresh ideas. The public school authorities themselves have gotten the message that their current forms of education aren't working very well. They have started new programs and are searching for alternatives within the system. In some cases, they have even turned to private organizations in their effort to reform local schools.

If we are going to form a new system, we need to be twice as creative. We need to start by enabling more and more parents to teach their own children at home. Resource centers should be developed where homeschoolers can share expensive equipment and band together for group instruction where appropriate. Private Christian schools should open their doors to part-time enrollment from homeschoolers. There also need to be more small private Christian schools. The ones that are already in existence must get out of their ruts and be open to new ideas and experiments. A means must be developed by which every Christian has access to an affordable church school. No one should be turned away because of monetary concerns. Every local congregation, no matter how small, should set up and subsidize a school for its own members. Parents should also band together to form small alternative Christian schools, or have "half-in, half-out" systems where they home school for part of the day and get together for the more difficult subjects or those that work better in group situations.

These issues will be explored in the final chapters of this book. Once again, it is not enough to read these suggestions and think about them. Now is the time for action. Whether inside or outside the public system, you can no longer sit back and allow others to make decisions for you. It is time for you to take back control of your children's education. Remember: The decisions you make (or don't make) and the actions you take (or don't take) today may have eternal consequences for your children!

Chapter 7

New Wine, New Wineskins

The idea for this book first came to me while I was working on *The Relaxed Home School*, which tells the story of our family's educational beliefs and practices. One day, while I was doing research at the library, I received a clear message from above. The Lord let me know that my next assignment was going to be for Him. He began showing me how much He dislikes what is going on today in the public school system of America, and how much He wants His people to change the face of education in this country. I was guided to a specific verse in the Bible, Ezekiel 17:24. It reads, *"And all the trees of the field shall know that I, the Lord, have brought down the high tree, have dried up the green tree, and have made the dry tree to flourish. I the Lord have spoken and have done it."*

    The Lord spoke to me through that verse and made it clear that He intends to uproot the high, green tree, the entrenched American public school system, and replace it with an entirely new system. The power will come from Him, but He needs us to be His workers. We must be the ones to set the wheels in motion so He can demonstrate His majesty to the unbelievers of the world.

It's time for most of us to stop focusing on attempts to change the old system. It is nothing more than a "used wineskin" and can never be fixed adequately. In Luke 5:36-39, Jesus talks about the foolishness of placing new wine into old skins. Pat Robertson has also discussed this issue in his book, *The Secret Kingdom*. When talking about the "law of change," he states,

> "Jesus is telling us that the spirit and message of the kingdom of God is always new, but that the receptacles prepared by human beings to receive it will age, become rigid and inflexible, and then must be replaced by receptacles that are new, pliable, and able to adapt. God is always the same; His plan is always the same. But the vehicles, the organizations, and the techniques of carrying out His program will always be changing." (p. 210)

The public schools of America have definitely become "old wine skins": rigid, inflexible, incapable of serious change. However, the problem goes even deeper

[handwritten in left margin: 8/19/01 Exactly why Joseph Smith and the restoration! was so necessary.]

than that, because they never were receptacles prepared by human beings to receive the message of God. Somehow, early in the history of this land, our forefathers goofed. They allowed themselves to be deluded by others who claimed to know what was best for their children. While they slumbered, Jesus was systematically removed from the school system, and His influence was eliminated from their children's education.

Barring another revolution or the "Second Coming," I doubt seriously that the secular mentality of this land will ever allow the public schools to return Jesus to his proper place at the heart of education. The foundations of a new system have already been laid. There are already many Christian churches, Christian schools, parent-run schools, home-schooling support organizations, and individual families who are working toward this end. We only need to build on those foundations and coordinate our efforts in order to complete the job and reach our ultimate goal. By ourselves, none of us has the power to create a viable system of Christian education strong enough to render the public system unnecessary. Together, with God's help, *"the things which are impossible with men are possible with God."* (Luke 18:27)

Part IV
What <u>Must</u> Parents Do?

Chapter 8
What are Our Obligations as Parents?

It's always a lot easier to point fingers and criticize what is wrong with something than it is to come up with creative solutions. The first time I started writing this section, I floundered for days. My divine inspiration seemed to fly right out of the window. Finally, I realized that I was approaching the subject all wrong. I had entitled this section, "What Can Parents Do?" rather than "What Must Parents Do?" The imperative has to be stronger these days, and I think God was waiting for me to remember that before He allowed me to proceed.

The first thing we must all do is to go back to the basics: not necessarily the "basics of education," but the "basics of life." Jesus must be returned to the center of our children's education. We must take control of our families again. Neither is an easy task, but life was not always designed to be easy.

A couple of years ago, there was a big workshop planned at Regent University, which is associated with Pat Robertson's Christian Broadcasting Network. It was called "Educational Options: Choosing for Your Child's Future." There were speakers lined up to discuss three possible options: public school, private school, and home-schooling. I was so excited, because I had been selected to be one of the key speakers on home education. Then, at the last minute, the entire seminar was canceled, due to a "lack of interest." At first, I couldn't understand it. I watched the "700 Club" all the time. I had seen the wonders of the "Founder's Inn" as it had been built and had heard all about the fantastic workshops that took place there. How could a conference on such an important topic be "canceled due to a lack of interest?" As usual, as long as I tried to figure it out on my own, I had no insights whatsoever. Finally, I took it to God, and asked Him. His answer came swiftly and plainly. It was canceled because He didn't <u>want</u> it to be held! Why not? Because the seminar was treating the three topics in too "balanced" a manner. God doesn't want us to make our choices based on a belief that home-schooling, public schooling, and private schooling are three equally satisfactory choices, because they aren't equally satisfactory to Him.

What are our responsibilities as parents? What does God really want for our families? He makes it clear in Deuteronomy 6:6-9 where He says, *"These words, which I command thee this day, shall be in thine heart, and thou shalt teach them diligently unto thy children and shalt talk of them when thou sittest in thine house, and when thou walkest by the way, and when thou liest down, and when thou risest up."*

It is now 7:15 in the morning and still quite dark. I was awakened fifteen minutes ago by a flashing light in the bedroom, and wondered for a minute what it could be. Then I realized that it was the school bus. Like many areas, our district is overcrowded, and the children must rise very early to catch the bus and be taken across the county to the nearest available school. They won't return until it is almost supper time. At that point, their parents will be coming home, tired and overworked. If they are like most parents these days, they will be lucky to clean up the house, get supper on the table, hassle the kids about their homework, and lay out the clothes for the next day. I doubt highly that anything scriptural will take place, except perhaps for a quick prayer at bedtime.

Did any of these parents talk of the Lord to their children this morning when they "rose up?" Or were they too busy trying to throw breakfast on the table in time to get to their respective jobs and busses? How about while they were "sitting in the house and walking in the way?" Many of these parents don't even return from work until supper time. One lady on my street comes home about 8:00 p.m. I know she has a daughter the same age as mine, but I've never seen the little girl except in the morning when she is waiting at the bus stop.

The question is, "Can today's children be instructed properly, as God has commanded, while both parents work all day and send them to a secular institution where they will be taught by other people, who may or may not share the parent's values?" The answer, unpopular though it will be, is "no." Even in a best case scenario, where the children are going to a Christian school and being taught by wonderful Christian teachers, it contradicts God's original plan for families. He put us together into such families because He intended for fathers and mothers to raise their children and instruct them in His Word themselves. He did not intend for families to separate every day, so fathers and mothers could go off and do something constructive out of sight of their sons and daughters. He wanted fathers to work close to home, where their activities and lifestyles could be seen by the most important people they will ever influence. From the little we know of Jesus' own childhood, it appears that his earthly father, Joseph, did his carpentry work close to home, where he could teach Jesus the trade. Mary was also around, sharing her faith with Jesus on a daily basis. This is the pattern most desired by God, but it has often been ignored, even by some of the great men and women of the Bible. King David erred when it came to this area of his life. Because he didn't share his faith enough with his own sons, he wound up losing Absalom to the enemy. His most successful son, Solomon, did an even worse job with his own family. He had so many wives, many of whom were pagans, that there was no way he could *"train up his children in the way they should go,"* (Proverbs 22:6) and he wound up breaking up a kingdom as a result.

God did not intend for mothers to look for fulfillment outside of their families and their homes, either. He wanted them right where He put them, attending to their households, raising and instructing their own children. Why do so many women today feel the need to search for fulfillment elsewhere? It's because they have given up the most exciting part of their job to outsiders! It's never much fun cleaning house, wiping noses, and doing laundry. Babies are wonderful, but life can be very lonely when the oldest is still in diapers. Just when the kids get to be old enough to be fun and to be helpful around the house, they are sent away for the best part of the day. Just when the adventure becomes challenging and the children are old enough to carry on intelligent conversations, they go away so others can share their discoveries and applaud their successes. At the exact moment when the walls could become less confining, mothers find themselves alone within them. No wonder so many women leave home. Everybody else has already gone!

In the following chapters, I'm going to discuss several educational options available to parents, but I'm not going to make the same mistake twice. I won't act like I'm talking about three equally acceptable alternatives. I won't hedge on what I believe is the best choice, what is the second best choice, and what I think is the worst option of all. However, I know that you all won't select door number one. As long as you take control of your own families, put

Jesus back where He belongs, and are comfortable with your own decisions, I'll be happy. Besides, it doesn't matter whether you make me happy or not. You know what really matters! So read on with an open mind and a willing heart and make your choices on your knees. Then you will know for sure that you have found the right answer for you. As the Bible promises,

"Ask and it shall be given you, seek and ye shall find, knock and it shall be opened unto you" (Luke 11:9).

Chapter 9

Is Homeschooling Right for Your Family?

Don't answer too quickly! You might be surprised. We didn't start out to be a home-schooling family, either. When Sam, our oldest son, was a toddler, I happily trotted him off to a mother's day out program every Tuesday and Thursday morning. At the age of three he was promoted to Mondays, Wednesdays, and Fridays, followed by a five day program at the age of four. The next year he marched off to kindergarten, and I have to admit I breathed a sigh of relief when the summer holidays were over and he was back in school.

We were living in Mississippi then, and there was no public school kindergarten available. The program in which he was enrolled was a Baptist preschool where there was very little emphasis on academics. He went to school to play while I stayed home with the baby and caught up on housework. Once in awhile, I had a few doubts.

Occasionally, he would look extremely tired and unhappy at the end of the school day, especially when I overdid it and left him there for "extended session." Whenever I picked him up early, I couldn't help but notice he was over in the corner by himself playing with blocks or trucks while the teacher had the rest of the children grouped around her listening to a story. It made me wonder if he was actually learning anything. At the time, though, I had thoroughly fallen for the idea that children needed certain group "socialization" experiences in order to develop properly. Even if he wasn't hanging around with the group, I thought maybe he needed to spend those hours in the company of his peers. After all, who was I to question a system that all my friends and neighbors believed in?

Sam was a precocious kid from the start. When he was six weeks old, the nurse at the doctor's office thought he was three months old. When he was two he could pass for four, due to his height and advanced vocabulary. He learned to read at the age of three and a half. Some of the other parents frowned when I told them he was reading books like *Charlotte's Web* by the time he was in kindergarten. "You shouldn't let him do that!" they said. "What will you do when he gets to first grade?" I always answered them in typical Scarlett O'Hara fashion. "I won't think about that today. I'll think about it tomorrow ..."

As the fateful day approached, we looked into an alternative school in Jackson. They were very individualized in their approach and encouraged parental involvement. It seemed ideal, but there was a catch. We were Clinton residents and would have to sell our house and move in order to participate in their program. Nevertheless, we signed him up for the waiting list and reluctantly started making plans to put the house on the market. We believed at the time that his schooling was worth a major disruption in our lives.

When the real disruption came, though, we found we weren't prepared. About a month before school was due to open, my husband's office was unexpectedly shut down and we were forced to move to Birmingham, Alabama. So much for the wonderful alternative school we had found. I had to start again from scratch in a new community, with less than a month left before the beginning of the school year.

Private school was too expensive. It was clearly not an option as long as I wanted to stay home with three-year-old Ginny and our new baby, Dan. I began looking into all the public schools in the Birmingham area. After narrowing down the possibilities and determining which was considered the best elementary school in town, I made an appointment with the principal and went for a tour of the facilities.

She proudly told me all about the "new" program that Alabama was then embarking on. It was called "excellence in education" and was designed to lift the public schools of Alabama up from their position near the bottom of the national school rankings. As she described the program, it gradually dawned on me that the program was going to result in the virtual elimination of play periods and class parties. Looking at my six-year-old my son, I realized that he was not ready for "excellence in education" if it meant staying on track academically for six hours a day. Like most boys of that age, he was just not ready for that "sit-down and be quiet" style of instruction all day long.

I told the principal about Sam's well-developed reading abilities. "No problem," she assured me. "We individualize all the children's reading programs." Try as I might, I couldn't get her to explain what she really meant by that, though. "What will Sam be doing all day," I asked, "while the other children learn the basics of reading?"

"Well, of course, it won't hurt him to go back over some of that material," she answered. "And we have a wonderful gifted program. If he tests into that in a few months, he can go off for some extra instruction two hours a week."

Well, I wasn't so sure Sam was "gifted," whatever that meant. I just knew that he loved to read and wouldn't want to sit around going over material he had covered three years ago. I went back home thoroughly frustrated and confused. I knew he would have real problems in that setting. Boredom and physical inactivity would cause him to turn into a behavior problem. Unless he had an awfully understanding teacher, his "creative" way of thinking might also cause disruption. I remembered his kindergarten instructor, a wonderful lady who was a friend of my husband's. One day the class was learning "f is for fish," and poor little Sam was almost in tears because he just <u>knew</u> they were wrong. Instead of dismissing his concern, the teacher questioned him further. It turned out that the fish in question happened to be a "gar," and Sam felt that it should have a "g" in front of it instead of an "f." The teacher told me later, "I didn't know it was a gar myself, but I <u>knew</u> that if Sam said it was a gar, it was a gar." Would another teacher care enough to notice things like that?

I went home and started to pray in earnest. It was Friday night. Sam was due to enter school the following Monday, and I still didn't have a clue about his proper placement. This was shortly after my serious "conversion" experience, and it was the first time I really turned my life over to the Lord for his guidance, holding nothing back. "Please help us!," I cried. "I need to know what you want me to do for Sam's education." At the time, I figured I'd be led to a different school or a different teacher. Well, I was led to a different teacher all right... me! For his entire education! It was probably just as well that I couldn't see the future at that moment. If I'd known then what I was really getting into, I'm not sure if I would have had the nerve to follow through!

On Sunday morning, I opened the newspaper and there, right on the front, was an article about a small group of parents who were homeschooling their children. The idea did not really appeal to me at first. I had known a homeschooler once, and I thought she was a little weird. Her daughter didn't seem to be able to get along with the other kids, and she was a real "granolatarian" type, always baking whole wheat bread and wearing granny dresses down to her ankles.

One thing about the article did strike home, however. It mentioned that Alabama law didn't require children to enter school until the age of seven. I had just assumed that my little six year old needed to go because everybody else his age was going. "Hallelujah!" I yelled, "Reprieve for a year."

Later that day, walking through the zoo, I turned to Sam and said casually, "How would you like to stay home with me this year?" He looked up with astonishment and delight. "Sure!" he answered. My husband, Roy, responded a little less favorably. He gave me a look that clearly said, "Lady, you have lost your mind."

He told me later that he went off the next weekend on a fishing trip, and spent the whole time walking around the lake muttering, "She's crazy. She's really, really crazy! She's lost it this time." It didn't help that the principal gave him a call to tell him that I was making a big, big mistake. I think she called him on purpose when she knew I was over at the school picking up Sam's medical records.

Luckily, my husband didn't really let me know how much he disliked the idea at the time. He knew I had a lot of knowledge about education and respected my ideas enough to give us a chance, even if he did think I was nuts. He believed we would be moving to a nearby small town soon anyway, and thought it was a temporary decision, made primarily in order to avoid a mid-year crisis. Little did either of us know then that Sam would remain a homeschooler (except for one minor detour in the seventh grade) until he finished his high school education.

Frankly, I don't remember when it first dawned on us that we had turned into a real homeschooling family. That first year, Ginny was supposedly "ready" for preschool, so I dutifully trotted her off three times a week, taking Sam and the baby back home. It didn't feel right to me. I hated to leave her there while the rest of us were doing interesting activities together. At that time, though, I still considered preschool a necessity, and she seemed to like it well enough.

As we suspected, we moved to a small town near Birmingham halfway into the school year, in order to enable me to finish a master's degree in education. At that time, my plan was still to have 2.5 children (well, maybe I'd keep the three I already had) and become a teacher as soon as the youngest was in "school." I hadn't really committed to homeschooling as a lifestyle at that point. However, I was feeling increasingly schizophrenic about having one child in and two children out, so I didn't enroll Ginny in preschool when we moved to the other town.

In the meantime, my husband was slowly being won over. He could see the increasing family togetherness. Several negative personality traits that had developed in Sam during the preschool years were starting to disappear now that he wasn't around so many rowdy boys. We had fewer colds, and the kids seemed very happy. There was no real shortage of friends or experiences for them to be properly socialized. About the only negative thing was the grandparent resistance factor. Roy's parents couldn't help but feel that we were denying the children something important. As former teachers, it was very hard for them to understand why we were taking such a drastic course of action.

As I started to read books and magazines about homeschooling and hook up with support groups, (which were much harder to find back then), we gradually realized we were not alone. Our original reasons for starting homeschooling were replaced by longer-lasting ones. By about the second or third year, it was apparent that we were in it for the long run.

Why did we decide to stick with it? In addition to our growing conviction that we were on the right track spiritually, we also learned to love the lifestyle. It was so flexible! We found we could pick up and go on family vacations during the "off" seasons without any crowds around and take field trips whenever we wanted. We could spend beautiful autumn days outdoors where the children belonged. It was much easier to remain in control of the family schedule, so the children could enjoy a "balanced" childhood: equal measures of work, academics, and creative pursuits, with lots of free time left for play. No late nights sitting up trying to finish homework assignments. No early morning races to get to the school bus stop.

Best of all, I got to know my children better and found out we actually liked being together! When Sam was in preschool, I couldn't wait to get him out of the house in the morning. During vacations, he hung around and acted bored. By the time the session started again, we were both eager to have him leave for a portion of the day. Now, with no "school" for comparison, our daily activities started to be more fun. I began to enjoy his company again. On nice days, we were able to go to the zoo or the park. I often wondered how he would have felt if he had been cooped up indoors at such times while the rest of us romped in the out-of-doors.

In the beginning, we heard about two or three sources for curriculum materials and dutifully sent off for a bunch of texts and workbooks, but they were tedious and none of us really liked them. The books were boring. We quickly set them aside and went back to what we did best... having a good time learning on our own. We went to the library once a week and Sam read everything he could get his hands on. He didn't seem to miss the "skills instruction" he would have been receiving in school. We took turns reading to the younger children. We put on plays and made tape recordings. We collected bugs and leaves and put up a bird feeder. We made a nature trail in the woods out back and created a guide book to go with it. The only formal instruction we had was in math, where we used a workbook series. I wasn't confident enough back then to make up my own lessons in that area. It amused me that Sam referred to math as "home school," because it was the only really structured lesson he did every day. Apparently, he thought that was the only thing that counted educationally.

My husband was thoroughly won over within a short time. He quickly saw the benefits of the home-schooling lifestyle, and within a year or two he was an ardent supporter. If he had remained adamant about wanting the children in school, I would not have continued. If we had not achieved unity, it might have caused a serious rift and that would not have been the proper thing to do. I'm just thankful that he was willing to give me an opportunity to change his mind!

These days, my friends often look at me and say, "How can you possibly home school now that you have five children?" I look at their lifestyles and think, "How can you possibly manage with all of your children in school?" At least I know that I'm the one in charge of our schedule and can arrange things so they remain in balance most of the time. I know who the children's friends are, and can monitor the influences they have on their lives. I know that we are following God's command to instruct them in keeping with His principles. I know they are fairly safe and that they feel secure and contented. Besides, I've had the delightful experience of watching first-hand as they have developed into wonderful kids with special talents and unique personalities. Of course, it hasn't been all sweetness and light. We've had our problems over the years, but we have managed to conquer them by pulling together as a family.

It has become increasingly difficult for me to "justify" homeschooling to people who come up to me at the grocery store to challenge our educational decision. Homeschooling has become such a mainstay of our lives that it is hard to even imagine why anyone else thinks it is unusual anymore. People ask the same questions, over and over. "But what about socialization...and college...and computers...and athletics...and this and that and the other thing." One of these days I'm going to turn to somebody, drop my jaw, open my eyes wide with astonishment, and ask, "Do you mean your children are school-schooled?" and see what they say. Sometime in the future, perhaps we'll be the ones with the "normal" educational choice and they will wind up as a small, insignificant remnant!

Chapter 10

"But, what about...?"

Once I had a friend who had three children. One was a preschooler and the other two were in the public elementary school. She was a real "dynamo," always busy and over-committed. Besides her responsibilities as a scout leader, she was a volunteer at the school and did art projects there every week. One of her children was having difficulties, however. This daughter was a very pretty girl and wound up attracting the attentions of all the "nasty" boys in the school. My friend spent half of her time in the principal's office trying to fix things that were broken. For every hour she spent there, she spent another hour rehashing the problems with her friends. She used to say, "I wish I could home school like you do. The problem is, I just don't have enough time." She didn't realize that she already spent many more hours on her children's education than I did homeschooling my kids! If she had dropped all the volunteering, homework assistance, and conferences with the principal and had just taken her children home and taught them herself, she would have had time to spare for all her other activities!

There are many reasons parents give for <u>not</u> teaching their own children at home. Most of them reflect a misunderstanding of what homeschooling is all about. Before I attempt to clear up these misconceptions, though, I want to emphasize again that the decision rests squarely in your own hands. You are the only ones capable of deciding what is best for your individual families. Therefore, despite my deep-seated convictions about homeschooling, I'm not going to tell you that you must make the same choice that I have or be deemed "unfit parents." I do hope that you keep an open mind so you are able to seriously consider the possibility should you ever feel the Lord is leading you in that direction.

The most common reason I hear for not homeschooling stems from a lack of confidence. Let's address this particular myth first. I can guarantee that you have what it takes to do the job. How can I say this categorically, without ever meeting you personally? First of all, because you are a parent, and you know your children better than anyone else on earth. Second, because the Bible says so. It promises that, *"With God, all things are possible"* (Mark 10:27). <u>All things</u>. That includes homeschooling, although it doesn't necessarily mean it will be easy. We were never promised life without difficulty or struggle.

Recently, a visitor to our home commented that I must be "very brave" to teach all five of my children at home. I don't think I'm all that brave! Sometimes, I get down-right scared when I think of the responsibility that we have assumed for our children's education. Whenever that happens, I remember that soldiers are often frightened when they go out to battle, too. They fight because they have received a command and they are obliged to obey. As soldiers in a spiritual war, we have to obey any directives that we receive from our Commander. If they seem harsh or impossible, we have to simply trust that we will be given the strength, tools, and circumstances that we need to carry out His instructions effectively. If you believe that the Lord wants you to try homeschooling, you can trust Him to provide whatever may be currently lacking. That includes the skills, knowledge, resources, and confidence to do the job properly. So if you are being led in that direction, go for it! Step out in faith, and don't give in to the fear that you will mess up somehow and ruin your children for life.

Other than the fear factor, the most common objection I hear is the perceived lack of "socialization" among homeschoolers. There are two related issues that come under this heading. First, people wonder if home-schooled children will wind up too sheltered because they don't meet enough people with different lifestyles and viewpoints. Second, they wonder if they will learn how to get along with others, and be able to avoid loneliness, especially if they have few siblings around.

I must confess that this was one of my own initial concerns. However, I quickly realized that my fears were unfounded. Our children have never had any trouble getting along with others outside of the family. A few years ago, for example, we joined a 4-H club. It met in the local elementary school and all of the other members were students there. That first night, our children didn't know anybody. By the time elections were held a month later, Ginny was elected president and Sam vice-president! So much for "having trouble getting along with their peers!"

In some ways, of course, home-educated children <u>are</u> more sheltered than others. After all, that's what it's all about! I consider it part of my business as a parent to shelter my children from negative influences when they are small. However, I also believe in exposing them to the outside world a little at a time as I believe that they are ready. For example, I would never read a book to my preschooler entitled, *Daddy's New Roommate*, about a homosexual relationship. However, when my teenage son wanted to participate in a dramatic presentation that included several homosexuals in the cast, I let him go. Of course, I also made sure that he realized the potential for harm and I was around enough to see that the production was well supervised. I let him go because I believed he was mature enough to handle the situation with a little help. It's all a question of timing.

It is certainly possible for homeschoolers to raise their children in too narrow a fashion, but most of the ones I know deliberately seek out interesting experiences for their children. They may participate in community theatre productions, sports leagues, or church-related organizations. They may do service work through church or volunteer at public places like the library or a local nursing home. We have never had trouble making sure the children had enough friends. They have been involved in so many groups and activities over the years that our biggest concern was keeping balance and avoiding the problems that go with being over-committed.

On the plus side, our children have learned to get along with people of different ages much better than most school children.   So many young people today have difficulty talking to adults. They also have few experiences with younger children unless they have little brothers or sisters of their own. Our children are equally at home with the elderly and the very young.   My fourteen-year-old daughter has two best friends.   One of them is seventeen and the other is eleven.   When I was in school, we used to think that we couldn't hang around with anyone unless they were our own chronological age, give or take six months. A "best friend" that was three years younger would have been almost unthinkable.

People also wonder if our children will ever be angry later because they think they were too sheltered, or missed out on certain experiences by not going to school. I remind such critics that some of the children who aren't sheltered now might wind up dead. Others will spend years going down the wrong road. I feel confident that our children will wind up making proper decisions and leading lives that are productive and fulfilling. However, I do make an effort to add in special experiences to substitute for the ones that they aren't going to have. Ginny may never dance at a prom, but she is currently working as choreographer on a community production. Sam may never work on a school newspaper, but he has already had his work published in a national magazine. Dan may never play on a high school sports team, but he has had plenty of opportunities in community leagues. My children may be missing some typical high school events and activities, but they are experiencing other things that will create lasting memories. They are all pleased to be homeschoolers, (at least most of the time), and I doubt seriously that they will feel any remorse about the situation later. If they do, we'll deal with that when it happens. I've never believed in worrying about the future so much that it interferes with the process of living today.

There are two groups of parents who are often particularly afraid to try homeschooling: those with "too many children" and those with "too few children." Those with one or two children sometimes worry that their children will be lonely. Those with a lot of kids are concerned that the presence of babies and toddlers will make it impossible to work adequately with the older children.

As far as babies and toddlers are concerned, they can certainly be a handful, but there are ways to manage. It might help to remember that teachers in school experience a lot of disruptions, too. You may have diapers to change instead of forms to fill out. You may be dealing with a disruptive two-year-old instead of a class clown. Good teachers everywhere simply do the best they can under whatever circumstances surround them. Sometimes, when life gets in the way of instruction, "formal" schooling might go down the tubes for awhile. Whenever I had a new baby, there were usually a few months when we didn't do much that looked very creative. However, the children were learning anyway! For one thing, they learned a great deal of patience by having to deal with their younger siblings. They also received practical experience in "child development." My fourteen-year-old daughter already knows more about that subject than most of the sophomores I used to teach at college.

If you have several young children, you might need to work with them as a group, rather than giving individual instruction. You can read books to them at "storytime," and go out with them on walks or make collections for science. If you focus on your long-range goals and remember that the early days of childhood will pass quickly enough, you will be able to teach a number of young children very effectively. If there are a couple of older children in the household who require a little individual instruction, one of them can baby-sit for the younger ones while you work with the other one. If there is just one older child and a bunch of little ones, you might need to get more creative. Perhaps you could hire a baby-sitter for a couple of hours once in awhile to get the time you need with the older student, or wait until your husband comes home and do a little schoolwork together in the evenings.

The problem of having just one child, or two or three widely-spaced children, can actually be tougher to solve. In this case, you will probably have to be willing to seek out extra experiences for your children or they may be lonely at home. Nowadays, most areas have active home-schooling support groups that sponsor a variety of children's activities. You can also make use of community programs, such as sports groups, art classes, or theatrical productions. You may have to make an extra effort to find friends for your children and arrange for them to come over to your house occasionally. If you make the effort, most of you will be able to overcome the problem. The only exception might be a person who lives in an extremely remote area and has an only child in the family. In that case, you may have to choose between sending your child to school for "socialization" or accepting the fact that he or she will lead a somewhat sheltered childhood in the company of adults. Worse things have happened.

On another level, people sometimes worry about homeschoolers "abandoning the public school system." While it is always nice to consider the welfare of others, in reality most parents make their decisions based on what they feel is right for their own families. That's only natural and proper. Bill Clinton didn't pause to consider what was right for the other children of the country when he made the decision to put his daughter in private school. We didn't consider the welfare of the other kids on the block, either, when we decided to teach our children ourselves. However, homeschoolers can certainly continue to be a positive influence on others in their communities. For one thing, the mere fact that they are at home most of the day doing interesting things and looking like they enjoy being with their children usually draws all the kids in the neighborhood to their door. That's one reason it's uncommon for homeschoolers to experience a shortage of friends or a lack of "socialization."

Homeschoolers can also remain active by making their voices heard at school board meetings and getting involved in local legislative activities. They can help Christian parents who are still involved in the schools fight controversial issues, like "Outcomes-Based Education." They can spend time volunteering at a local school (if their own children are old enough to accompany them), or offer to donate used materials to the school library. They can work with other children through their local churches. These are all appropriate ways for homeschoolers to continue to minister to the other children of the community.

I don't believe, however, that it is appropriate for parents to expect young children to "minister" to other children on their own, without adequate adult supervision. Several people have told me they would like to be homeschoolers, but they believed that their children could do more good by going to public school and witnessing to the other students. That sounds good on the surface, but young children are much more likely to be swayed themselves than to serve as a "point of light" for others to follow. Some high school students may be mature enough to accomplish such a task, but even they will have a tough enough job keeping their own values straight in the face, of heavy peer pressure. Expecting anything more may be a bit unrealistic, except in unusual cases.

Another common reason given for not homeschooling is the need for both parents to work full-time. Sometimes, this is a legitimate concern. Before children can be adequately educated, they must certainly be housed and fed. However, there are other cases where parents have simply allowed a "credit card" mentality to take over their lives. It may be necessary for some of you to sit down and ask yourselves some hard questions concerning your priorities. Many parents in the homeschooling movement were originally full-time workers, too, but they have rearranged their priorities and their schedules in order to be at home with their children. Some of them have started "at-home businesses" or "down-sized" their jobs to fit the home-schooling lifestyle. Others have worked split shifts so that one parent could work while the other stayed at home. Still others have been able to revamp their lifestyles so they could make it on a single income. Few homeschoolers are really well off by the standards of the world. Many parents have only one car or a smaller house than they would like. They use coupons and buy their clothes at consignment shops. They look for free educational opportunities and buy used books or rely entirely on the public library for their curriculum materials. These parents have learned that their increased freedom and control far outweigh the things that they have had to give up.

What if you are a single parent? Is homeschooling a possibility for you? Again, the Bible tells us that anything is possible! I've got to admit, though, that this might be a little tough to manage. However, there are single people who have done it quite successfully. Some of them have traded in their outside jobs for home businesses, or have started day cares in their basements. Those with younger children have sometimes hired baby-sitters or tutors for part of the day. Sometimes they have been able to find teen-aged homeschoolers who were willing to help with younger children during the day. Those who have older children have learned to trust them to remain on track without constant supervision. I'm sure it isn't easy, but the rewards may be worth the trouble. It isn't easy to deal with all the problems associated with public school attendance, either. If you do choose to try, there is help available. In addition to your local home-schooling support group, there is a national organization for single parents who teach their own children at home. They have a newsletter where they share ideas and support each other. The address is included at the back of the book. It certainly must be a challenging lifestyle!

As for me, I am very grateful that my own husband earns a good living. It would be very difficult to feed our family and meet all our needs without his steady income. I sympathize with those of you who really must work all day outside the home in order to keep the wolves away from the door. If you absolutely can't homeschool, you need other choices to explore, too. In the next chapters of the book, we're going to discuss some other possible solutions. Whatever you do, though, don't give up! The Lord will help you provide a Christ-centered education for your children one way or another, if you just ask Him for his help.

Chapter 11

What About Private Schools?

When our forefathers first arrived on this continent, education was considered to be the responsibility of the church. The entire rationale offered for the building of a school in the Plymouth colony was the need for young children to learn to read the Bible. A Christian education at a small private school is certainly the next best thing to home-schooling. In some cases, it may even be preferable, if the parents are unable, incapable, or unwilling to attempt to teach their own children adequately. Such an education should be readily available to every family in America.

When we were trying to decide where to place Sam, long before we ever thought about homeschooling, we explored the public school arena exclusively, searching for that special teacher, principal, or program that would be right for our son. We didn't give private schools much consideration. Our reasons were partly financial and partly philosophical. We weren't rich then, and we aren't now. I wanted to stay home with my younger children, and knew that we could not afford a private school education on my husband's salary. Also, every Christian school that I had heard about seemed to operate under a particular educational philosophy, using similar methods and materials. Since I didn't share this highly-structured, textbook-oriented view of education, and we didn't happen to be rich, private school was out of the question from the start.

If it was out of the question for us, it probably is for a lot of other parents as well. If we are going to completely replace the decaying American public school system with a new system of private education, it must be capable of serving everyone who wants to participate. Private Christian schools have to be available, affordable, and palatable to every Christian in the country. Private non-Christian schools also need to be built to meet the needs of people who do not share our faith. Since there is a wide range of religious and educational belief systems present among American families, there must be a broad assortment of Christian and secular schools available, so that appropriate matches can be found for everyone.

In this chapter, I'm going to discuss some of the reasons that our family didn't feel comfortable with the available choices, in the hopes that a few additions or modifications might make some private Christian schools more attractive to those who share my concerns. I hope that private school administrators and church committee members read the following with an open mind.

1. My sons do not have close-cropped hair, and my daughter has a very special sense of fashion which is not compatible with tartan plaid skirts, white blouses and black string ties.

Over the years, I have often picked up catalogues from private schools, wondering what I would do if homeschooling ceased to be an alternative. While I'm a great believer in having a well-disciplined student body, I also believe strongly in the importance of celebrating our unique personalities. It seems to me that most Christian schools do everything they can to make sure each child looks and acts like a clone of his peers.

I have a hard time believing that students have to wear uniforms in order to behave themselves properly or take school seriously, or that the boys really need to wear ties and have their heads shaved above the ears. What does any of that have to do with true discipline? True discipline is an internal affair, and is developed over time, under the guidance of adults who demonstrate respect for their students, have consistent expectations, and enforce rules fairly. Sure, it may be easier for the teachers to manage behavior if everyone looks and acts the same. That's what they teach in secular "behavior modification" courses, too. We're not supposed to be behaviorists. We're supposed to be Christians and Christians are supposed to value individuals. Herding techniques may work, but that doesn't make them right.

Of course, in the absence of strict codes, teachers might have to deal with an occasional short skirt or low-cut blouse, or a spat among covetous children who are jealous of somebody's shoes. If the teachers do their best to deal with such situations, and are backed by parents who care and a principal who will enforce a reasonable disciplinary code, they will have little trouble. The children also need to learn how to cope with such situations. If they are always taught that life is black and white, they won't learn how to deal with the gray areas. They can't begin to exercise their own judgement if they are always told exactly what to look like, act like, and think like. As adults, we don't all dress and act exactly alike when we go to work, so why should we expect children to do so? Can't we trust them a little bit more, and give them the chance to live up to our high expectations?

Back in the fifties and sixties, when I went to school, we had a dress code, too, but administrators didn't attempt to eliminate all individuality. Filthy sayings weren't tolerated on t-shirts, and suggestive blouses or short skirts were sure to merit a trip to the principal's office. There's nothing wrong with a basic dress code that requires the students to live up to certain standards, but my children would never go to a place where their individuality is stifled as much as most Christian schools demand.

2. I hate textbooks. Even before they were dumbed down to suit today's readers, I hated textbooks. Even when they are written by Christian publishers, I hate textbooks.

Textbooks are almost always boring. They skip over interesting subjects and condense entire wars into two paragraphs. The science texts might as well be written in another language. Textbooks cover topics in very superficial ways, and rarely hold enough interest to spark any child's enthusiasm for a subject. The children go through the texts, learning just enough information to spit it back on an exam, and then promptly forget everything. I know. I was the world's best learner and forgetter. I did it for over twenty years, in pursuit of two master's degrees and a Ph.D. My own children have turned into voracious readers, mainly because I haven't turned them off by boring them to death. They will never go to school where textbooks drive instruction, and that describes the curriculum of almost every Christian school I've ever seen.

3. I want balance in my children's lives, and I want to retain control over the family schedule during the hours the children are at home.

My son's best friend for several years went to an elite private Christian school. In the summertime, they played together every day. They were virtually inseparable. However, as soon as fall hit, Sam could forget about spending any more time with his friend, because his friend spent every single night parked in front of a mound of homework. I don't think that quality education should require three hours of homework a night on top of what goes on inside the classroom all day long. When that is the requirement, something is wrong somewhere. Either an enormous amount of time is being wasted somehow in the classroom, teachers are not coordinating their requirements adequately, or somebody is a big believer in busywork. Personally, I believe in childhood. Kids need time to play, to think, and to rest. They also need time to spend with their families and time to contribute to the work load at home, learning responsibility from their parents. They don't need to go to school all day long and then come home with an armload of books to occupy them all through the evening and into the weekend. Such requirements take all control for the children's lives away from the parents and the children themselves. Their entire lives are then controlled by outsiders. My kids would never go to school anywhere unless the teachers and administrators understood this need for balance, and allowed my husband and me to control the family schedule after school and on the weekends.

4. Christian schools are not immune from problems with abusive behavior, peer pressure, drugs, and violence. I want my children raised in an atmosphere of safety, where Christian values and behavior patterns are the norm, not just a far-off goal.

Because many schools solicit and accept students who are not necessarily Christians themselves, many of the same problems found in the public schools can be found in Christian schools, too. This will always be the case as long as these schools view evangelism as one of their main goals. Winning souls is a wonderful task, but I'm not sure it is an appropriate emphasis in a place that is supposed to be devoted to the provision of a Christian education to the members of the congregation and the community. I think school administrators should ask themselves, "What is our primary task?" and then devote themselves to it. To me, the primary task should be serving the needs of those Christians who are looking for a truly distinctive Christian environment. This means eliminating any disruptive pupils, even if their souls are thereby placed in danger and their money is removed from the church coffers. The church itself can provide necessary outreach to such families, but I don't believe such children should remain in the school if their ideas, values, and behavior patterns seriously compromise the provision of a distinctly Christian education to the children of the congregation.

5. Last, but not least, we aren't rich, and I didn't want to go out to work while my other children were still preschoolers. We couldn't afford any of the private Christian schools I knew about, so they would never have been an option, even if the rest of the criteria for a quality education had been met.

This is the toughest problem of all. Making Christian schools affordable to everyone will require creative solutions. It will also require a spirit of "giving" on the part of Christians who do not have school-aged children of their own. Every single church should have a small school set up to serve their own congregation. When a church isn't available or responsive, individual parents should band together and set up their own Christian school. That's the way things worked in the early days of this country. If we all provided for our own, there would be no need for gigantic government bureaucracies or federal regulations and red tape.

There are several ways to make education more affordable for those who are participating. To begin with, costs must be cut. There is no real need for the expansive facilities that are often considered a prerequisite for setting up a "school." A quality education can take place in a structure that doesn't have a gym or an auditorium. The early Christians in this country certainly didn't sit in air-conditioned comfort, in well-lit halls, and take their recreation in state-of-the-art gymnasiums. When the first step in building a school is to take out a huge mortgage on the facilities, a certain measure of control has been given away before instruction can even begin. All that is really needed for a quality education is a roof over one's head, an enthusiastic, committed teacher, and a responsive student. It is not necessary to wait to start a school until the money has been raised for a million-dollar facility! You can begin with what you already have and trust the Lord to provide the money for materials and expansions as they are really needed.

Of course, a major part of the budget for a Christian school is taken up with salaries for teachers and administrators. It's no secret that many of these people are already underpaid and do their work for love, not money. However, there are ways to cut back on some of these costs, too. One skilled administrator, carefully chosen and given a free hand by the church elders, can do more than several semi-competent administrators wearing handcuffs. Only a few full-time teachers are really required. Larger class sizes don't have to be a negative factor, provided that the slack is taken up by parent volunteers. This does not have to be a mere pipe dream. However, in order for this to work, there must be a change of heart on the part of the parents and educators involved. True commitment and a spirit of cooperation must be present on both sides. Parents must be willing to come in and help. Teachers and administrators must realize that they are actually secondary players, acting in the role of servants to the parents. At the very least, those parents who want to participate must be considered equal partners in education. They need to be given real responsibility for instruction and planning and serve as actual instructors, not just sit in the back of the room grading papers. They must be viewed as an important part of the school team, and be invited to conferences and workshops to develop their own professional skills. They must be included in the decision-making process. It is not enough to have a token parent representative on the planning board.

Parents, in turn, need to realize that their selection of a private school does not exempt them from their responsibility for participating in their children's education. If they allow their professional commitments to overshadow their commitment to their own children, something is out of whack. Every one of them can make some kind of contribution of time and talent, even if some of those contributions must take place after hours.

Of course, parents are not the only ones who have responsibilities to their children. All of the members of the congregation are supposed to be concerned with the task of raising and educating the next generation of Christians. These others have important roles to play, too. To begin with, they must be willing to help foot the bill for the education of the children of their own church, even if they don't have school-aged children themselves. In addition to money, they need to be willing to contribute their own time and talents to the effort. There are many older people in the community who have worthwhile things to share with children. They can teach them useful skills, add spice to the study of history by relating personal tales, and provide needed companionship. If nothing else, they can sit and listen to the children talk. For some children today, the lack of adults who will listen is a major concern. Young people, single or married, can also be a valuable resource in the school. They can learn a great deal themselves by spending time with children before making the decision to start families of their own. If they are busy during the hours school is actually in session, they can volunteer for after-school recreational programs or fund-raising activities.

In addition to finding ways to hold costs down, Christian schools need to start looking for better ways to raise funds, too. Somehow, they must lessen their dependence on tuition as the major source of funds. High tuition is the biggest factor in keeping many parents out of private schools. Anyone with a head for business knows that real money can't be made selling candy or holding bazaars and car washes. Without some kind of serious fund raising effort, all the real money is going to have to come from the pockets of the parents. There needs to be an entrepreneurial spirit in the Christian education world. Every school should consider starting a side-business, where the older children learn valuable job skills while making some real money for the institution. The businessmen in the church need to put their heads together and think of ways to accomplish this. The widow's mite may be a wonderful gesture, but it won't bring the cost of private education down enough to make things affordable for everyone.

One possible way to hold tuition down to reasonable levels might be to use a sliding scale, based on a form of barter. Those parents who have more money than time can go ahead and pay high tuition rates. The others can bring their tuition down by earning points through volunteering at the school, thereby helping the administrators save money on professional salaries. Those who want to help, but can't do so during normal school hours, might be able to assist with office work in the evening, do work for the school's "side-business," or contribute other needed services or materials.

Some of you probably believe that I have my head in the sand, or am being unreasonably optimistic about the suggestions I'm making right now. Maybe you're right. I'm not an expert on private schools. But there has to be some kind of effort to bring down those high tuition rates. There has to be a way to do it, because God says anything is possible! If you think these suggestions are unworkable, come up with some different ones. We have to get creative, or our efforts to forge a new system of Christ-centered education will be doomed from the start.

****

Chances are that our family would have chosen home schooling anyway, even if there had been another option that we liked and could afford. However, it would have been nice to have a choice. Even if I could magically change every private Christian school in the country into one that we could afford and would like to participate in, I wouldn't do it, though. I know there are some parents who like uniforms and love textbooks as much as I hate them. There are probably some students who prefer short hair, and love tartan plaid. Somewhere out there, there may even be a few Christians who are rich enough to afford high tuitions! If students shouldn't all be clones of each other, neither should Christian schools. They don't all need to have similar policies, use the same materials, and have identical methods of instruction. As long as Christ is at the center, parents are in control of their families, and the Scriptures are taught as an integral part of education, there can be many variations.

One of the best ways to make sure a wide range of choices is available is to demand complete local control of schools, and give the parents a big voice in decision-making. That's true in both the public and private school sectors. Nowadays, there is a lot of talk about "school choice." Many people believe that the way to make private school affordable is to get the government to come in and provide the funds. In one way this makes sense. Taxation in this country has turned into little more than "legalized stealing." It pains me to know that my tax money is being squandered by people who couldn't keep a family or small business solvent for a month using the same practices. It sure would be nice to get some of that money back to use for my own children's education. However, I know from experience that whenever the federal government starts handing money out, strings rapidly become attached and entangled and everybody gets bogged down in red tape, bureaucracy, and secular regulations. Christ winds up fading from the picture completely.

Luckily, we <u>already</u> have school choice! That's what is still great about America. In many countries, this book would be totally useless. In such places, parents have no choices available to them and no hope for taking control, short of a revolution. Luckily, we still have the opportunity to make our own decisions. If we wait until the government steps in to make things easy for us, we will have to live with the new rules and regulations that follow. Chances are, our choices will actually wind up being more limited in the long run.

Chapter 12

Private Schools and Home Schools:

Partners in Education

If we are really going to form a new system of education, rather than a hodge-podge network of individuals, families and small schools, there is going to have to be a strong sense of commitment and community on the part of all Christians that are involved in the effort. There is always power in numbers, and strength in unity. Only together can we accomplish a task as large as the one that looms before us.

There is already a lot of cooperation going on. For example, the Christian home-schooling support organization that I have joined in Georgia has several hundred families that are participating. Last December, we went to a "school performance" of the Nutcracker Suite in downtown Atlanta. Our group had more students in attendance than any of the public school groups who were there that morning. We had been given the best seats in the house at a fraction of the usual cost. This home-schooling organization also sponsors sports leagues, art classes, and a band and chorus program for its members. But such support organizations need places to meet, and access to laboratories, sports facilities, and educational materials. They can't function adequately without some assistance from area churches and Christian schools.

In some states, where the private school laws are rather vague, homeschoolers are legally able to sign up with Christian schools, who allow the parents to act as "satellites" of the private schools. In addition to legal coverage, many of these Christian schools provide access to their facilities as well. Often, the home schoolers have a regular day of the week when they go to the school and have educational programs and a time for fellowship.

There are some other church schools that actually allow part-time attendance for home-schooling students. Just this week, I received a brochure in the mail from one Christian high school. Our ninth-grade daughter had heard about a school in this vicinity that enrolled homeschoolers on a "per class" basis, and was interested in taking courses in biology and ancient history. When the materials arrived, she took them out eagerly, only to find that the classes each cost $100 per month, in addition to registration and lab fees. Most homeschooling parents are making it on a single salary, and can't afford that level of tuition. Such programs are going to have to charge lower fees for such services if they really hope to attract home-schooling families in their community.

As usual, the cooperative spirit must be felt on both sides. Private school administrators and teachers must be assured that home-schooling families are willing to support their programs, too. The parents must be willing to contribute their own time, talent, effort, (and a reasonable level of money), to the church in return for the use of their facilities. Of course, everyone involved would need to be willing to bend rules where necessary. In some cases, the parents could only come in and help if they were allowed to bring younger children along. Although that might make for a few logistical problems, it would create a "family atmosphere" in the church school, and could even turn out to be a blessing.

Christian educators also have roles that they must play in getting this system off the ground. In many states, the law allows certified teachers to provide yearly evaluations for home-schooling families, which can either supplement or take the place of standardized testing programs. Some professional educators might also provide consulting services to families, diagnostic and referral services for children with special needs, and educational workshops for parents or students. However, such professionals will need to adopt a "servant mentality" if they are going to be viewed as helpful partners, instead of money-grubbing leeches.

Every year, I go to Pennsylvania to conduct "evaluations" for fellow home schoolers. These evaluations are required by law, and there is a great need for professionals who understand the home-schooling situation. It would be easy for me to charge large fees, to act like a hot-shot, and to fall into the role of "supervisor." However, I truly believe in the concept of parental control of education. I keep my fees reasonable, and never try to force new ideas on the parents, even if I think something should really be changed. My role is not to usurp other parents as "principals" of their home schools. I am merely the "go-between," a facilitating link between the parents and the public school administrators.

In order for this new system to grow, we must all pitch in and do our share willingly, whether we are professional educators, church deacons or pastors, laymen, parents, or members of the congregation. If every church makes the decision to provide an affordable school to serve its own members, and also provides legal coverage (where possible) for area home schoolers and invites them to participate part time in their programs, then the goal will be reached in a short time. Those parents who are able to home school will do so, feeling confident that any perceived deficiencies in their programs will be addressed through cooperation with the private school. Those who want a private Christian education will go to the church school. Those who desire a "half-in, half-out" program can do part of their teaching at home, and send their children to school half days. In this manner, every single Christian child in the United States can be provided with a Christ-centered education.

Of course, if we succeed in our mission, detractors will accuse us of tearing down the fabric of American education. They will be wrong. We are not the ones who are tearing down the public schools. That is happening without any help from us. It is their own foundations that are faulty, and with or without a positive solution from our side, they are doomed to slide downwards into decay. We are not interested in tearing them down further. We are interested in building up a new structure to replace something that is already dying.

But what will happen to the rest of the children of America, those who are not in Christian families or served by Christian schools? Some of them will begin to be served by the new secular private schools that have already begun to spring up all over the country. For a long time to come, however, there will be students who remain in the public system for one reason or another. Many of these public schools will be decayed, blighted structures where little light can possibly shine. However, others will feature new solutions thought up by the secular school reformers. Many will be entertaining, educational, and attractive. They will undoubtedly be "politically correct," but they will never be "spiritually correct." Still, some of the more creative programs will thrive, at least in the short run. And wherever possible, Christian teachers and parents can continue to exert small positive effects if they believe that their particular assignment is to remain and serve in the public sector.

As usual, the people who will be hardest to reach and serve adequately will be those from the most disadvantaged segments of society: the poor, the unemployed, the homeless. Christian churches must continue to reach out to the children from these families, too. Perhaps some of them can be brought into the new Christian school system through the use of church tithes, as long as they are either Christians or their behavior can be conformed to Christian standards. A few of these families might be able to become home schoolers, if adequate assistance could be provided by people willing to set up and man home-schooling resource centers in the inner cities. Yet even I have difficulty believing that the majority of them will be able to escape the public system for a long time to come.

What can be done to continue to serve those who must attend public schools? Are there any proper roles for Christians to continue to play on that battleground? These issues will be addressed in the next chapter, "The Role of Christians in Public Education."

Chapter 13
The Role of Christians in Public Education

At the start of each chapter of this book, I went to the Lord in quiet time and asked, "What do you want me to say next?" This morning, I again asked, "What shall I say about the public schools?" The answer was a simple one-liner. "You've already said it." I wanted to write something helpful for those of you who will decide to keep your children in the public schools. Unfortunately, I could receive no further insights, other than a renewed warning that the children will be on a dangerous battleground if they are allowed to remain.

In any war, there are many such battlegrounds. In order to win the war, it must be fought on all fronts. It is never strategically wise to give away a single battle without fighting. Therefore, there are certainly roles for Christians to continue to play in the public education sector. However, a dangerous war is no place for children. First, you must make sure your own family is safe. Only then can you be free to go out and fight yourself. It makes no sense to hand your own children over to the enemy and then turn around and focus on saving others.

For teachers or administrators whose children are grown or properly protected in a Christian environment, the public school is still an appropriate place to serve. As long as there is one child left in that system, the public schools should not be completely abandoned by Christian adults. Under the legal constraints that now apply, however, such teachers will face many situations where they have decisions to make. Unless there is an occasional opportunity for sharing their faith with the students, there is little of real value that they can accomplish. There will be times that Christians must be willing to put their jobs on the line in order to do or say something that simply must be done or said. There will be other times that more subtle, "life-style witnessing" will be sufficient.

Christian teachers should also make sure they are aware of the political views of any professional organizations to which they belong. Barring a revolution in the N.E.A., the largest teacher's union in America, it does not seem appropriate for a Christian to be a part of this organization, due to the radical social agenda that the leaders have adopted. There is a new, fledgling teacher's organization that many Christians are joining across the nation, instead. It is called, "The Christian Educator's Association International," and its address can be found at the back of the book.

Parents without educational credentials can also play a part in this battle. Those with children in private or home schools should not simply sit on the sidelines, but should roll up their sleeves and go to work alongside public school parents. They can band together to fight controversial issues, such as "Outcomes-Based Education," or attempt to influence the selection of textbooks and videos by the school board. In some cases, they may be able to serve on school boards themselves. There have been several cases where home-schooling parents have won such seats, and there is always room for Christian candidates for other legislative offices. Just this morning, there was a big article on the "Christian Coalition" in the Atlanta paper. This is a large political organization for Christians that helps people keep up with issues and encourages participation in voting and running for office. Politics can seem like a "dirty profession" at times. However, if Christians refuse to participate, the major decisions in this country might often be made by people who are being used by the other side.

Another organization that has been making a big difference is the American Center for Law and Justice, based in Virginia Beach. This group of lawyers has been waging a fairly successful fight to regain the rights Christians have lost in the public sector over the past twenty years. They can use our financial support as well as our assistance as "watchdogs" in our own communities. Anytime we notice a situation where the rights of Christians are being violated, we must be prepared to take a stand and "call in the troops." It is precisely the lack of involvement of the majority of Christians over a long period of time that has caused the current mess. This book was never meant as a criticism of the teachers, administrators, lawyers, and pastors who have been working for the reform and renewal of the public school system. They are fellow soldiers in the war, and although their assignments may be different than mine, we are all in this thing together.

As Christians, we must do what our own guidance tells us to do. For me, that has meant homeschooling my own children and writing this book. Only you can know what is best for your own families. Always remember two things. First, you are the parents, and therefore you are the only earthly experts that really know what is best for your children. Second, you have access to all the wisdom of the ages, and the power, intelligence, and strength to do whatever is in His will. As God has said, *"I am the Lord, the God of all mankind. Is there anything too hard for me?"* (Jeremiah 32:27). With His help, there is nothing too hard for you, either. In the last chapter, and the worksheets that follow, you're going to be given some concrete help so you can begin to take back control of your children's education. Wherever the quest leads you and your family, I wish you luck and will be praying for your success. And always remember to fight your battles proudly, knowing that the victory has already been promised!

"At the sign of triumph, Satan's host doth flee.

On then, Christian soldiers, on to victory.

Hell's foundations quiver, at the shout of praise.

Brothers, lift your voices, loud your anthem raise!"

(from the hymn, "Onward, Christian Soldiers")

Part V
On to Victory!

Chapter 14
Regaining Control

The very first step in regaining control over your family is to figure out what you believe about life and education and set a few goals. Without goals, you will never know where you are going, or be able to assess your progress along the way. If you have reached this point in the book without throwing it away, you are probably a committed Christian whose spiritual beliefs are similar to my own. This chapter deals with the importance of clarifying your educational beliefs, not your spiritual ones, although the latter are certainly more important in the long run.

Many Christians think that everybody who agrees on spiritual matters will automatically agree on educational issues as well. That just isn't true. Naturally, our beliefs and practices in the area of education are rooted in our spiritual beliefs. As Christians, we all share certain basic goals and values. That's one of the reasons you felt the need to read this book. Deep down, you probably already realized that your spiritual beliefs were being violated in the public school arena. However, there are important differences in educational philosophies within the Christian community as well. No two Christian schools are exactly the same. Their atmospheres, methods, and materials reflect the tastes and beliefs of individual headmasters and teachers, as well as the specific doctrines of their church founders. Within the homeschooling movement, there is also a great deal of variety when it comes to educational beliefs and practices, even among Christians who share the same basic values and goals for their children.

I like to think of the family of God as a large tree. Believers have deep roots, which help to stabilize them in every area of their lives. The tree has many branches, however. Just because we share a common bond, it does not mean our families are all going to look or act the same. Some families are more structured and "straight-laced." Others are freer and more easy-going. Some families exercise extremely tight discipline over their children. Others believe in a looser structure. Some parents are interested in the sciences, while other families tend to be more "artsy." In some, the father's primary role is to be the breadwinner and the mother's responsibilities are at home. In others, these roles may be shared or even reversed. There are also families that are headed by single mothers or fathers who are trying hard to hold things together in the face of difficulties and hardships.

God has built tremendous diversity into this world. Every snowflake has a different crystalline structure. No two zebras have the same pattern of stripes. If God places such a high premium on individuality in nature, why would He suddenly change character and expect all Christians to be clones of each other when it comes to their ideas about running their families? Must we all have exactly the same beliefs about discipline, the same styles of teaching or learning, and always agree on the methods and materials we use in order to qualify as "true Christians?" Of course not. There is only one thing necessary to be called a child of God. Our salvation does not hinge upon our choice of textbooks or unit studies or whether or not we believe in testing or grading our children.

However, there is at least one thing that is necessary for all of us, regardless of our educational preferences. If we want to exercise a higher level of control over our children's schooling, we need to do a little "homework" ourselves first. This is true whether we decide to teach our children at home or remain in private or public schools. After all, we can't "take charge" of something if we don't know anything about the subject ourselves!

Consider what would happen if you decided to go into the kitchen and bake cookies before you knew anything about the process. What if you didn't understand how to set the oven temperature or timer, and couldn't read the instructions because you weren't familiar with the terms? You could try to bake the cookies anyway through trial and error, but the results might be pretty interesting!

Similarly, if you want to succeed at taking charge of your children's education, you need to think and study a little about the subject first. You must learn a few educational terms and give some thought to current educational controversies. That doesn't mean you have to become an expert! After all, you don't need to become Julia Child in order to bake cookies for your family. You don't need a teaching degree before you can work with your own children, either. You don't have to feel uneasy about speaking out at a school board meeting just because you have fewer "credentials" than the people on the board. You do need to be knowledgeable about the subject, though, or you will not be taken seriously.

Figuring out your own "philosophy of education" is not as difficult as it sounds. For one thing, you already have one, whether you realize it or not! You have spent many hours in the educational system yourself as a student. You know a lot about how you learned, what teachers helped you, and why. You know what subjects you took and what percentage of that material has been retained or forgotten. You know what wound up being useful in "real life" and what turned out to be mere "academic pap." All you need to do is to think seriously about some of these issues so you can figure out what will be best for your own children.

It is important to remember that your basic assumptions about education were forged in the schools you attended as a child. For most of you, these beliefs were formed in a secular group setting. They may or may not be appropriate assumptions for you to hold today, especially if you decide to work with your children at home.

Examining such assumptions is probably the most critical step toward clarifying your own educational beliefs. Be an "assumption buster!" Figure out what you believe about the process of learning. Consider where your ideas originated and decide which ones you want to keep and which ones might need to be changed.

You must also think about the process of learning itself. How does learning actually take place? What does it mean to "learn" something? Is it enough to study material for a test and forget it within a week or should the results be longer lasting? Consider what you can do as a parent to help motivate your individual children to engage in "real" learning that will improve the quality of their lives forever.

After you work through your spiritual beliefs and ideas about learning, you must set some appropriate educational goals for your children and consider the relationships and roles that you think are appropriate for teachers and students. If you decide to teach your children at home, you will need to decide which methods of planning, instructing, and evaluating you are going to use, and select your educational materials. The worksheets at the end of this book will help you in this process of thinking through your educational philosophy. It is absolutely critical that you go through these exercises if you are considering homeschooling. If you don't want to actually write out the answers, at least think them through carefully in your head. If you are interested in learning more about the variety of educational philosophies that exist, and want to receive a little extra "help," you can read another book I've written, called *Countdown to Consistency*. It explains four educational philosophies that have influenced the home-schooling movement, and provides workbook pages that will help you figure out your own educational beliefs and form a plan of action for your own home school.

For those of you who are not planning to teach your children yourselves, it is still important to consider what you would do if you were completely in charge. Having a clear set of educational goals for your children will make it easier for you to recognize differences in philosophy among the teachers in your children's school and let them know why something strikes you as inappropriate for your family. If you can explain your beliefs to the authorities and point out the differences between their beliefs and your own ideas about education, they may be inclined to take your suggestions more seriously.

One of the biggest sources of disagreement among parents and school authorities is in the area of educational goals. This has been brought into sharp focus recently because of the controversy surrounding "Outcomes-Based Education." Obviously, the secular authorities who have shaped this plan have a different agenda than many Christian parents. Most Christians don't believe it is the job of the public school to work with their children in areas outside traditional academic pursuits, especially since the public school authorities have made it clear that they are going to do this in the absence of Judeo-Christian standards of morality. If you would like to learn more about this issue, you might be interested in reading a new book by Cathy Duffy, one of the leaders of the home-schooling movement, entitled *Government Nannies*. There is also an information booklet published by Concerned Women of America called, *Outcome-Based Education: Remaking Your Children Through Radical Educational Reform.* Ordering information for both of these books, as well as the *Countdown to Consistency* workbook mentioned above, can be found in the appendix.

Before entering into such controversies, it is important that you know what your <u>own</u> goals for your children are, especially your long-range goals. Having such goals will make it easier for you to compare your goals with those advocated by others. You will also have a valuable tool that will help you assess your children's progress, recognize any gaps that are developing, and make plans to address them.

I like to think of each of my children at the age of eighteen and ask myself the following questions: What do I want my children to believe? What sorts of values and attitudes do I want them to have? What kinds of habits will make their lives run more smoothly? What skills will they need? What specific talents should be encouraged and developed? What knowledge must they possess in order to be ready to go out into the world as effective citizens and "Christian soldiers"?

Back when the Iraq crisis started, there was a lot of hoopla about the lack of "geographical literacy" on the part of American students. Educators moaned and criticized the students because so few of them knew where Iraq was located on a map. Frankly, I didn't care whether my kids knew where Iraq was or not. I was able to make this distinction because I had already thought out what my own educational goals were for them. What did I care about? I wanted them to be concerned about the welfare of the people who were involved on both sides of the war. I wanted them to recognize that they didn't know where Iraq was and to be eager to take out a map or globe to find out. I wanted them to go to the encyclopedia to learn more about the history of the area without being asked. I wanted them to have enough background knowledge and academic skills to be able to look up this information and assimilate it on their own. Above all, I wanted them to love reading and learning about new things, so that they would continue to have such experiences all through their adult lives.

Whatever your goals are for your children, it is important for you to clarify them and help the kids learn to set a few goals of their own. Without such goals, the children will lack purpose and will drift aimlessly until they find someone else who will tell them what to do. They will thus be extremely susceptible to the influence of those who do possess goals. In the absence of clear direction from you, they may be swept up by someone with an alternate agenda and end up turning from your teachings. Isn't it worth it to put some time into thinking things through, setting some goals and making a few plans while you still have the opportunity?

The worksheets that follow are designed to help you in this process of taking back control over your children's education. To begin with, you need to outline your educational philosophy, and assess your current situation.

You need to consider the strengths and weaknesses, personalities, and interests of your children, and how these characteristics will affect your decision. You need to set some worthwhile goals so you can assess the progress that is being made toward them. You need to weigh the positives and negatives of homeschooling, private schooling, and public schooling, and make the decision where to place your children. It's time to take out your number two pencils and begin. I promise not to clock you or assign grades! (It would be contrary to my own educational philosophy to do so!)

Action Worksheets

The following worksheets are designed to help you assess your current educational situation and make the best choice for your family. It is very important that you consider the following questions and think about your answers. If you don't have the time or inclination to actually write down the answers, don't worry! It is probably just a sign that you are an "auditory" learner, and "write" best in your head!

Action Worksheet #1

Outlining Your Own Educational Philosophy

A. What are the basic spiritual beliefs that guide your educational ideas and choices?

B. What do you believe about the nature of learning? What are some of the assumptions about education that you developed during your own school experience? What worked for you as a student and what didn't work? What material was retained and proved helpful in your life as an adult, and what did you forget or find useless?

C. What do you think the the proper roles and relationships should be among teachers and students? If you choose to become a home-schooling mother or father, how do you think your role as a teacher will be different than your role as a parent? (Or will it be the same?)

D. If you decide to home school, what methods of instruction do you think would work best for your family? (Possible examples - reading together, doing active projects or "unit studies"*, going to the library, lecturing or conducting group discussions, arranging apprenticeships or outside learning experiences, etc.)

*Note: A "unit study" is an integrated approach to learning. Rather than studying disjointed subjects, like "math," "social studies," "language arts," and "science," the students study a particular topic, like "dinosaurs," or "volcanoes," or "American Indians." The other subjects, such as reading, writing, science & social studies are incorporated into the unit, using a combination of methods that include "active learning."

E. What kinds of materials would you select if you decided to teach your children at home? (Examples - good books from the library, magazine subscriptions, textbooks or workbooks, unit studies from publishers, self-made unit studies, etc.)

154

F. (For people who are not going to home school)

How do the views of the teachers and administrators
at _____ school line up with your own
views as expressed above?

What are the areas of agreement?

What are the areas of disagreement?

Action Worksheet # 2

Assessing Your Current Situation

A. Your child

(This should be done for each child individually)

What are some of your child's strengths?

Spiritually

Emotionally

Physically

Educationally

What are some of your child's weaknesses?

Spiritually

Emotionally

Physically

Educationally

What are your child's special talents and interests?

What motivates your child? What are some of his or her favorite subjects, and why?

What does your child like best about his or her current educational situation?

What does your child dislike about his or her current educational situation?

What are some of his/her own goals for the future?

B. Mother/Father

(It would be best to do two separate sheets, one for each.)

What are your own strengths and weaknesses?

Strengths:

Weaknesses:

What are your special interests and talents? How can you share them with your children?

What are your own goals for the future? How will they affect your educational choice?

Action Worksheet # 3

Your Educational Goals for Your Children

(This is important even if you do not become their teacher. If you have your own goals clearly spelled out, you will know whether or not they are being addressed by the teachers in your child's school. A different sheet should be filled out for each child.)

When my child is eighteen years old, I would like the following goals to be accomplished in these areas:

Values: I want my child to have adopted the following values:

Attitudes: I want my child to have developed the following attitudes:

Habits: I want my child to have developed the following habits:

Skills: I want my child to have learned the following skills:

Life skills:

Academic skills:

Special Talents & Interests: I want my child to have the opportunity to develop the following special talents:

Knowledge: I want my child to be knowledgeable in the following areas:

Action Workshop # 4

Choosing an Educational Option

If you are still trying to figure out what would be best for your family, write down all the perceived advantages and disadvantages of each of the following options.

Home school:

Advantages

Disadvantages

Private School:

Advantages

Disadvantages

Public School:

Advantages

Disadvantages

Action Worksheet # 5

Starting to Home School

What are the laws of your state concerning home schooling?

(To find out, either look up the law yourself at the library, contact your state organization or the Home School Legal Defense Association, or read *The Home-Schooling Resource Guide & Directory of Organizations,* a booklet I've written that can be found in many public libraries.)

What are the ages for compulsory attendance in your state?

(Read the law for yourself, or contact your state home-schooling organization to find out. If your children do not fall within these ages, it is not necessary to do anything to comply with the law.)

Are you required to notify the authorities in your state before you begin homeschooling? What are you supposed to send in, where and when?

(Ask your state organization or the Home School Legal Defense Association. Do <u>not</u> rely on information provided by the school board. Sometimes they add requirements that are not actually in the law.)

What is the address of your state support group? (See appendix.) Is there a local affiliate in your area? What kind and degree of support can you realistically expect to receive from this organization?

What material are you going to read to learn more about homeschooling?

(It would be best to subscribe to at least one home-schooling magazine, and read a number of the books that are listed in the "recommended reading" list.)

What changes are you going to have to make in your lifestyle to accommodate homeschooling? Are these changes possible? How are you going to accomplish them?

What are your potential strengths as a home-schooling parent? What are you particularly good at? What types of learning do you enjoy yourself? What are your special interests?

What are your own potential weaknesses as a home-schooling parent? What can you do to address these weaknesses?

What additional skills do you believe you will need to develop in order to perceive yourself as "competent" to work with your children? How are you going to develop them?

What materials are you going to use to start with?

(If you don't know, try to attend a curriculum fair in your area or talk with other home-schooling parents to get some ideas.)

Action Worksheet # 6

Choosing a Private School

____ Is it Christ-centered?

____ Do the teachers and administrators view parents as equal partners in education?

____ Do you agree with the educational philosophy of the instructional staff?

____ Do you agree with the religious doctrines of the church that sponsors the school?

____ Do you agree with disciplinary procedures?

____ Do you think that your children will be happy and safe in this school?

____ Do you think that they will have their individual needs met?

____ Do you think they will have opportunities to develop their unique talents and interests?

____ Is the school located near by? If not, how will the children get to and from school?

____ Do you agree with the school's policies concerning homework?

____ Can you afford the tuition at this school?

____ Is there a contract that must be signed? Do you have to pay an entire year's tuition "up front"?

____ Is there any provision for "bartering" or bringing down tuition by volunteering at the school?

____ Is there any provision for part time attendance and part time teaching at home?

____ Is there a program for participation by home schoolers in case you ever decide to "switch"?

Action Worksheet # 7

For Those Who Decide to Remain in the Public Schools

___ Do you know your children's teachers personally? What are their spiritual beliefs?

___ Have you read your children's textbooks and viewed any videos they are watching while at school?

___ Do you pray for your children every day while they are at school?

___ Have you joined the P.T.A and demonstrated your desire to become more involved in the real educational process at your child's school?

___ Do you keep up with controversial issues in education, especially those that are currently being debated by the local school board?

___ Do you make your voice heard, by attending school board meetings or writing letters to the newspaper on issues that matter to you?

Appendix A

National Organizations

General Information:

American Center for Law and Justice
P. O. Box 64429
Virginia Beach, VA 23467
(804)579-2489

> Legal defense for Christians involved in major
> lawsuits

The Christian Coalition
Box 1990
Chesapeake, VA 23327
(804)424-2630

> Lobbying and information service for Christians
> involved in the political process

The Christian Educator's Association
P. O. Box 50025
Pasadena, CA 91115
(818)798-1124

> Christian teacher's organization, alternative to
> N.E.A.

Concerned Women of America
P. O. Box 65453
Washington, DC 20035
(202)488-7000

> Lobbying and information service for conservative
> women, Christian emphasis. Call them to order the
> booklet, *Outcome-Based Education: Remaking
> Your Children Through Radical Educational
> Reform.*

Home Run Enterprises
16172 Huxley Circle
Westminster, CA 92683
(714)841-1220

> Write or call for information on ordering the book,
> *Government Nannies*, by Cathy Duffy. Also
> publishes *The Christian Home Educator's
> Curriculum Manual*, which is an excellent source
> for learning about the variety of curriculum materials
> that are available.

William J. Murray Evangelical Ministry
P. O. Box 803312
Dallas, TX 75380
(214)242-1198

> Organization dedicated to restoring prayer in public
> schools.

Home-Schooling Organizations:

Home School Legal Defense Association
P. O. Box 159
Paeonian Springs, VA 22129
(703)338-5600

> Membership-based legal insurance for
> home-schooling parents

Home School Legal Defense Association of Canada
202-Dunmore Centre
1601-Dunmore Road S.E.
Medicine Hat, Alberta T1A 1Z8
(403) 528-3400

> Legal insurance and information for Canada

The Relaxed Home Schooler/Ambleside Educational Press
P. O. Box 2524
Cartersville, GA 30120

> This is my own organization. I publish a free
> quarterly newsletter for homeschoolers who prefer
> loosely-structured curriculum materials and
> methods. If you fall into that category, feel free to
> write and ask for a free subscription. I also have a
> mini-catalogue of supplies, and am willing to answer
> specific questions if possible, as long as they are
> submitted in writing, rather than over the phone. (I
> need to continue doing a good job with my own
> kids, too!) Write for ordering information on
> *Countdown to Consistency*, *The Relaxed Home
> School*, and, of course, *Onto the Yellow School Bus
> and Through the Gates of Hell.*

National Challenged Homeschoolers Association Network
5383 Alpine Road, SE
Olalla, WA 98359
(206)857-4257

Organization of parents teaching special needs
children at home

Single Parents Educating Children in Alternative Learning
2 Pineview Drive, #5
Amelia, OH 45102

Organization for single home-schooling parents

Appendix B

Recommended Reading

General:

Concerned Women of America, *Outcome-Based Education: Remaking Your Children Through Radical Educational Reform.* Available through CWA, address in Appendix A.

Duffy, Cathy, *Government Nannies,* 1995. Available through Home Run Enterprises. Address in Appendix A.

Deals with the issue of government control of education and interference in family life.

Macaulay, Susan S., *For the Children's Sake: Foundations of Education for Home and School,* 1984 . Crossway Books, Wheaton IL.

This is my own favorite book on education. Deals with the issue of respecting children and valuing their intelligence.

Home Schooling:

Duffy, Cathy, *Christian Home Educator's Curriculum Manuals*. Two volumes. Elementary manual, 1995 edition currently available from Home Run Enterprises, 16172 Huxley Circle, Westminster, CA 92683. Jr/Sr High manual 1995 edition due out about June, '95.

One of the best curriculum guides available. This book can help you locate the materials that will be best suited for your family.

Harris, Gregg, *The Christian Home School.* Brentwood, TN: Wolgemuth & Hyatt, 1988.

Explains the problems currently found in the public schools from a Christian standpoint. Discusses first steps in starting the home schooling process.

Hood, Mary, *Countdown to Consistency: A Workbook for Home Educators,* 1992. (Available from Ambleside Educational Press, P. O. Box 2524, Cartersville, GA 30120).

Explains four educational philosophies found within the movement; designed to help home educators clarify their ideas about learning and translate their goals into a workable educational plan for their family.

Hood, Mary, *The Relaxed Home School,* 1994. Cartersville, GA: Ambleside Educational Press (address on previous page).

Provides practical help for home schoolers who desire to move toward a less structured, flexible approach to education.

Klicka, Chris, The Right Choice: *The Incredible Failure of Public Education and the Rising Hope of Home Schooling.* Available from the Home School Legal Defense Association. See address list.

Wade, Theodore Jr. and others, *The Home School Manual,* 6th ed. Auburn, CA: Gazelle, 1995.

One of the most comprehensive works on the subject. Includes several articles from other authors. Christian perspective.

Home-Schooling Magazines: (1995 subscription prices)

(Canadian subscribers: Please remit in U.S. funds, with either a money order or a check drawn on a U.S. bank or write directly to magazines asking for guidelines.)

1. *Growing Without Schooling*
    2269 Massachusetts Ave.
    Cambridge, MA 02140
    Subscriptions: $25.00/year (6 issues) $28 in Canada

    This is a secular magazine. However, it appeals to some Christians who believe in loosely-structured educational methods and materials. Some of the materials sold through their book store may be considered inappropriate for Christians.

2. *Home Education Magazine*
    P. O. Box 1083
    Tonasket, WA 98855
    Subscription $12.00/6 months (3 issues) or
    $24.00/12 months (6 issues) $33.75 Canada

    Another secular magazine. However, there is a wide spectrum of religious beliefs and educational methods represented, including Christian ones. Articles, helpful lists, advertisements.

3. *Home School Digest*
    P. O. Box 575
    Winona Lake, IN 46590
    Subscription: $15/year (4 issues) $18 Canada

    Christian perspective. Informative articles and essays.

4. *Home Schooling Today*
P.O. Box 1425
Melrose, FL 32666
Subscriptions: $20.00/year ($16 pre-paid) (6 issues)
$27.00/year ($24 prepaid) in Canada
Canadian checks and m.o. must have
9-digit American routing number

Christian perspective. Emphasis on practical ideas,
many using "unit" approach.

5. *Practical Home Schooling*
P. O. Box 1250
Fenton, MO 63026
Subscription: $15/year (4 issues); $25 for 8 issues
(Add $10 in Canada)

Christian perspective. Emphasis on computer use
and curriculum reviews.

6. *The Teaching Home*
P. O. Box 20219
Portland, OR 97220-0219
Subscriptions $15.00/year (6 issues) $20 Canada
Christian perspective. Contributors tend to believe in
highly-structured, subject-oriented educational
methods and materials.

Special Interest Newsletters

(Send S.A.S.E. to get info and current rates.

1. *Catholic Home School Newsletter*
    688 11th Ave. NW
    New Brighton, MN 55112

2. *Home School Court Report*
    (legal info from HSLDA)
    P. O. Box 159
    Paeonian Springs, PA 22129

3. *Home School Researcher*
    c/o Western Baptist College
    5000 Deer Park Dr. S.E.
    Salem, OR 97301

4. *Jewish Home Educator's Newsletter*
    (SASE ($ .52) for sample
    Ernstoff
    2 Webb Road
    Sharon, MA 02067

5. *Patriarch*
    (Christian homeschooling fathers)
    601 Madison
    Arnold, MO 63010

Appendix C

State Christian Home-Schooling Organizations

(Note: These organizations change address often, since they are frequently based in the current leader's home. If you are reading this after 1995, I'd suggest you contact "The Teaching Home Magazine" for a current list, or find a current copy of either *The Home-Schooling Resource Guide & Directory of Organizations,* or the latest version of Ted Wade's *Home School Manual* in the library. When writing to these organizations, please include a self-addressed, stamped envelope with extra postage.)

Christian Home Education Fellowship of Alabama
P. O. Box 563
Alabaster, AL 35007
(205)664-2232

Alaska Private and Home Educator's Association
P. O. Box 141764
Anchorage, AK 99514
(907)696-0641

Arizona Families for Home Education
P. O. Box 4661
Scottsdale, AZ 85261-4661
(602)941-3938

Arkansas Christian Home Education Association
P. O. Box 4410
North Little Rock, AR 72116
(501)758-9099

Christian Home Educator's Association of California
P. O. Box 2009
Norwalk, CA 90651-2009
(800)564-2432

Christian Home Educator's of Colorado
1015 S. Gaylord, # 226
Denver, CO 80209
((303)388-1888

T. E. A. C. H. of Connecticut
25 Field Stone Run
Farmington, CT 06032

Delaware Home Education Association
Box 1003
Dover, DE 19903
(302)653-6878

Florida at Home
4644 Adanson St.
Orlando, FL 32804-2024
(407)740-8877

Georgia Home Education Association
245 Buckeye Lane
Fayetteville, GA 30214
(404)461-3657

Christian Homeschoolers of Hawaii
91-824 Oama St.
Ewa Beach, HI 96706
(808)689-6398

Idaho Home Educators
P. O. Box 1324
Boise, ID 83680
(208)482-7336

Illinois Christian Home Educators
P. O. Box 261
Zion, IL 60099
(708)662-1909

Indiana Association of Home Educators
1000 N. Madison, # 52
Greenwood, IN 46142
(317)638-9633

Network of Iowa Christian Home Educators
Box 158
Dexter, IA 50070
(800)723-0438

Christian Home Educators Confederation of Kansas
Box 3564
Shawnee Mission, KS 66203
(316)755-2159

Christian Home Educators of Kentucky
691 Howardstown Road
Hodgenville, KY 42748
(502)358-9270

Christian Home Education Fellowship of <u>Louisiana</u>
Box 74292
Baton Rouge, LA 70874-4292
(504)642-2059

Homeschoolers of <u>Maine</u>
HC 62, Box 24
Hope, ME 04847
(207)763-4251

<u>Maryland</u> Association of Christian Home Educators
Box 3964
Frederick, MD 21701
(301)663-3999

<u>Massachusetts</u> Homeschoolers Organization of Parent
Educators
15 Ohio St.
Wilmington, MA 01887
(508)658-8970

Information Network for Christian Homes <u>(Michigan)</u>
4934 Cannonsburg Road
Belmont, MI 49306
(616)874-5656

<u>Minnesota</u> Association of Christian Home Educators
P. O. Box 188
Anoka, MN 55303
(612)753-2370

<u>Mississippi</u> Home Educators Association
109 Reagan Ranch Road
Laurel, MS 39440
(601)649-6432

Missouri Association of Teaching Christian Homes
307 E. Ash St. # 146
Columbia, MO 65201
(314)443-8217

Montana Coalition of Home Educators
P. O. Box 43
Gallatin Gateway, MT 59730
(406)587-6163

Nebraska Christian Home Educators Association
Box 57041
Lincoln, NE 68505-7041

Home Education & Righteous Training (Nevada)
P. O. Box 42264
Las Vegas, NV 89116-0264
(702)593-4927

Christian Home Educators of New Hampshire
Box 961
Manchester, NH 03105-0916
(603)647-1463

Education Network of Christian Homeschoolers of New
Jersey
65 Middlesex Road
Matawan, NJ 07727
(908)583-7128

New Mexico Christian Home Educators
5749 Paradise Blvd NW
Albuquerque, NM 87114
(505)897-1772

New York State Loving Education at Home
P. O. Box 332
Syracuse, NY 13205
(315)468-2225

North Carolinians for Home Education
419 Boylan Avenue
Raleigh, NC 27603-1211
(919)834-6243

North Dakota Home School Association
4007 N. State St.
Bismarck, ND 58501
(701)223-4080

Christian Home Educators of Ohio
P. O. Box 262
Columbus, OH 43216-0262
(800)274-2436

Coalition of Christian Home Educators of Oklahoma
P. O. Box 471032
Tulsa, OK 74147--1032

Oregon Christian Home Education Association Network
2515 NE 37th St.
Portland, OR 97212
(503)288-1285

Christian Homeschool Association of Pennsylvania
P. O. Box 3603
York, PA 17402-0603
(717)661-2185

Rhode Island Guild of Home Teachers
Box 11
Hope, RI 02831
(401)821-1546

South Carolina Home Educator's Association
P. O. Box 612
Lexington, SC 29071
(803)951-8960

Western Dakota Christian Home Schools (South Dakota)
P. O. Box 528
Black Hawk, SD 47718-0528
(605)787-4153

Tennessee Home Education Association
3677 Richbriar Court
Nashville, TN 37211
(615)834-3529

Home-Oriented Private Education for Texas
P. O. Box 59876
Dallas, TX 75229
(214)358-2221

Utah Christian Homeschoolers
Box 3942
Salt Lake City, UT 84110-3942
(801)394-4156

Christian Home Schooling of Vermont
2 Webster Avenue
Barre, VT 05641-4818
(802)476-8821

Home Educator Association of <u>Virginia</u>
P. O. Box 1810
Front Royal, VA 22630
(703)635-9322

<u>Washington</u> Association of Teaching Christian Homes
2904 N. Dora Road
Spokane, WA 99212
(509)922-4811

Christian Home Educators of <u>West Virginia</u>
P. O. Box 8770
S. Charleston, WV 25303-8770
(304)776-4664

<u>Wisconsin</u> Christian Home Educators Association
2307 Carmel Avenue
Racine, WI 53405
(414)637-5127

Homeschoolers of <u>Wyoming</u>
P. O. Box 926
Evansville, WY 82636
(307)237-4383